MW00588380

THE
DEVOTIONAL
FOR
Black
Women

52 Weeks of **Affirmations**, **Bible Verses**, and **Journal Prompts** to Strengthen Your **Spirituality** and Embrace **Black Girl Magic**

CHELSEA LA'NERE BROWN

ULYSSES PRESS

Published by:
Ulysses Press
PO Box 3440
Berkeley, CA 94703
www.ulyssespress.com

ISBN: 978-1-64604-611-9
Library of Congress Control Number: 2023943929

Printed in the United States by Kingery Printing Company
10 9 8 7 6 5 4 3 2 1

Acquisitions editor: Kierra Sondereker
Managing editor: Claire Chun
Developmental editor: Sasha-Gay Trusty
Editor: Renee Rutledge
Proofreader: Sherian Brown
Front cover design: Aderice Palmer-Jones
Interior design: what!design @ whatweb.com

*To my son, Cannon, the driving force behind my
journey after God's heart.*

CONTENTS

INTRODUCTION

Black Girl Magic is really a thing! God has instilled something special within Black women that must be nurtured, embraced, celebrated, and shared with the world. In order for Black women to walk boldly in our magic, however, we are required to have deep intimacy and oneness with God while growing in our faith and relationship with Him.

Black Girl Magic is a special brand of spirituality and sisterhood that allows us to call forth our authentic selves by learning to live unapologetically in who we are. It's our divine inheritance made for us when we were created in His very image. Black women have the opportunity to become unique contributors to the Kingdom of God. It is God who calls us to this. However, we often face barriers that make it difficult for us to recognize the true essence of the calling and purpose of our lives.

This is where our relationship and intimacy with God come into play. The truth of our identity lies in the hands and heart of the one who created us. It is in His image that we were designed, so coming to know the depths of God's core reveals to us our unique makeup. Reclaiming our self-image not only fuels our self-confidence and worth, it also equips us with the ability to fulfill the destiny God strategically planned for our lives. When you know who you are, you understand the importance of your existence. Your purpose becomes clear when God can trust that you—the you HE called you to be—will fearlessly embrace your divine assignment.

This devotional is a tool for weekly reflection, awareness of your God-given power, building intimacy with God, and growth as a Christian woman. It is also a tool that will empower you to push past societal influences that we, as Black women, often allow to limit our identities; and instead embrace the identity given to us by God. This opens the pathway for God to reveal our purpose and calling.

This devotional will minister to your soul, renew your thoughts, and enliven your spirit. So, let's awaken your faith in Christ's ability to reveal who He has created us to be. Walk proudly and boldly in His will for your life.

HOW TO USE THIS DEVOTIONAL

This devotional provides practical biblical principles and inspiration to empower Black Christian women to build intimacy with God, to embrace our identities in Christ, to identify our God-given purpose, and to walk confidently in our calling.

This devotional is split into three parts: Identity, Purpose, and Calling. Unearthing your identity in Christ is the foundation for discovering your life's purpose and walking in your calling. As you journey through the three biblical principles in this devotional, you will walk away more confident in the who (identity), why (purpose), and what (calling) as it relates to your walk with Christ. You will become more empowered, equipped, and confident in your spiritual walk and using your Black Girl Magic to embark on your heavenly assignment. Each week contains one Bible verse, one devotional lesson, and one reflective thought or activity such as:

❀ a biblical affirmation
❀ a journal prompt
❀ a prayer
❀ a weekly homework assignment (e.g., meditate on this week's Bible verse for 10 minutes per day)

The weekly Bible verse is designed for you to meditate and reflect upon while also building familiarity with God's Word. Throughout this devotional, I use Bible verses from the New Living Translation (NLT), the

New International Version (NIV), the English Standard Version (ESV), and The Message (MSG). The version selected for each week is based upon the vernacular and what would be more comprehensible for the reader and the devotional message.

The weekly devotional messages provide context to the scripture and how it relates to your walk and growth with Jesus Christ as a Black woman. The corresponding reflective activity encourages practical application of the week's scripture and devotion. So, be sure to thoroughly engage with each portion of the week's lesson to experience the full benefits of combining God's Word, biblical wisdom, and real-life application that will empower a spirit of boldness and cultivate closeness with God.

The weekly devotionals are undated to allow you the freedom to engage at your leisure. However, it's best practice to start the weekly devotional at the beginning of the week (Sunday or Monday), as many of the reflective activities call for participation throughout the week.

True spiritual growth and life transformation are results of the intentionality we put into prioritizing our time and relationship with God! Therefore, it helps to schedule a specific day and time of the week to complete the weekly devotional to build consistency and your commitment to this journey. You can do this by putting your time with God on your calendar, setting a weekly/daily alarm, or recruiting an accountability partner.

Part 1

Identity

Dear Black Girl Magic...

SCRIPTURE

Thank you for making me so wonderfully complex! Your workmanship is marvelous—how well I know it. *Psalm 139:14 (NLT)*

DEVOTIONAL

God took his time creating us. Every day we continue to defy the odds and achieve everything society once said we couldn't. This was no mistake by God. From NASA to the classroom, Black women have continued to excel and shatter glass ceilings while setting our own standards of beauty, business, and everything in between. We often refer to this as our Black Girl Magic. Black Girl Magic speaks to our confidence, strength, and independence, which is natural to us. These characteristics are things we are born with. We could be born without sight, hearing, arms, or hands and still have that magic within us.

One day while journaling, I decided to write love letters to Black Girl Magic. I wanted to acknowledge and celebrate the complexity and uniqueness given to us by God. So, on a sheet of paper, I wrote:

Dear Black Girl Magic,

Failure is not an option! The only way we fail is if we give up! Taking breaks and giving ourselves grace is totally acceptable. Because let's face it—our magic can get messy at times. But quitting is NOT allowed! There may be turbulence, layovers, bumps, and detours on the journey, but we must stay the course!

Dear Black Girl Magic,

Together with God, we are unstoppable. The creator gifted me with you to help me live my purpose out loud! So, there are two very important things I want you to remember:

1. With God, we can conquer anything we set our intentions on.

2. Because of God, we already have! The victory is already won (1 Corinthians 15:57), and nothing or no one can do anything about it!

Dear Black Girl Magic,

We have only just begun! I know it has been a wild ride thus far, but we have not reached our peak. There is so much more in store. Eyes have not seen, and ears have not heard all that awaits if we just keep pushing through!

REFLECTION

We all have Black Girl Magic inside of us. Write a letter to that Black Girl Magic. What do you want it to know about your past, present, and future?

_____

_____

_____

_____

_____

_____

_____

_____

_____

_____

_____

_____

_____

_____

_____

_____

_____

_____

_____

_____

Allow Me to Reintroduce Myself...

SCRIPTURE

I praise you, for I am fearfully and wonderfully made. Wonderful are your works; my soul knows it very well. *Psalm 139:14 (NLT)*

DEVOTIONAL

If you had to stand in front of a small crowd of strangers and introduce yourself, what would you say? Would you identify yourself as a wife? Mother? Friend? Would you begin to detail your profession and/or passion? What about your interests, hobbies, and things you like to do on the weekends?

My guess would be yes to all of the above.

From the moment we enter the world, our earthly identity begins to take shape. Our families, environment, and societal influences begin to mold us into who we ultimately grow to be. As adults, we tend to identify ourselves by our roles, titles, interpersonal relationships, and careers. Black women are often falsely identified by our appearance, strengths, weaknesses, and socio-economic status. But time and time again, we forget that our true identity rests in Christ and who He intricately and divinely created us to be.

Our heavenly identity and who God called us to be is where our real power and purpose lie. It is what will drive you to show up fully in the roles assigned to you on Earth. It is what makes you beautiful. It is what makes you, well, YOU!

REFLECTION

Below are biblical affirmations that will help you begin to reframe your mind around your spiritual identity. Repeat these affirmations to yourself each day this week to experience a true transformation of the mind!

Affirm:

I am fearfully and wonderfully made. (Psalm 139:14)

I am gifted for greatness. (1 Corinthians 12: 4–7)

I am empowered to accomplish God's will. (Ephesians 1:17–21)

I am a crown of glory. (Proverbs 12:4)

I am God's masterpiece. (Ephesians 2:10)

I am the Lord's own treasured possession. (Malachi 3:17)

I am a child of God. (John 1:12)

A Woman's Work

SCRIPTURE

She is clothed with strength and dignity, and she laughs without fear of the future. *Proverbs 31:25 (NLT)*

DEVOTIONAL

The Bible makes clear the importance of a woman's role on Earth. God created women to be helpmates, encouragers, and givers of life. We are wives, mothers, sisters, and friends. We continue to break barriers and shatter glass ceilings as homemakers, CEOs, world leaders, and much more.

In recent years we have become our strongest advocates for change and equality through social justice movements. Additionally, we have countless biblical examples of strong women, like Mary, Rachel, Hannah, Ruth, and Queen Esther, defying the odds and being chosen by God to complete miraculous works.

Despite all the wonders that come with being a woman, society has often made us feel less than and incapable as we maneuver through womanhood. For many of us, it's hard to admit that we struggle with the feminine identity given to us by God. We are afraid that the things that make us women disqualify us from being warriors for God. We do not think it is okay to depend on God for protection or provision, and we spend more time trying to prove our strength than we do trying to rely on His.

The bad thing is that our culture mocks us for our femininity and praises us when we display masculine energy. Thankfully Jesus has already restored the compromised identities of His people, and He does not expect us to fight this battle of reclaiming our womanhood alone.

Oh sweet Daughter of the King, it is time to reclaim our God-given identity as we usher in a new era of the Kingdom of God.

REFLECTION

Recite this prayer over yourself and every woman in your life:

Heavenly Father, you are the masterful creator of everything that makes me a warrior woman in your Kingdom. Father, thank you for creating me to be virtuous in your likeness and strength. Grant me the ability to balance the softness of my femininity and the boldness to fight against the plots and schemes of the enemy. May I walk my path of womanhood fearlessly and faithfully as the woman you created me to be! In Jesus's name, amen.

Mirror, Mirror

SCRIPTURE

She is more precious than rubies; nothing you desire can compare with her.
Proverbs 3:15 (NLT)

DEVOTIONAL

I'm sure many of us have heard the saying, "Comparison is the thief of joy." Well, it's true! In a world where we constantly consume the highlight reels of family, friends, and strangers across media outlets, it's becoming increasingly difficult to dodge the comparison trap.

Between social media, news outlets, magazines, and "reality" television, standards for success and beauty have risen to, oftentimes, impossible and unrealistic heights. But would you believe that the spirit of comparison didn't start with the media? Nope! In fact, the comparison trap swept through generations dating back to biblical times.

Let's head over to the book of Genesis and take a look at the story of sisters Rachel and Leah, for example. Both women, who were married to Jacob, struggled with comparing themselves to one another. Rachel, seemingly infertile, grew bitter toward Leah, who was able to bear Jacob several children. On the other hand, Leah compared her worth as a wife by the abundance of love and affection Jacob showed Rachel, and not her.

With each child Leah birthed, she hoped and prayed Jacob's love for her would grow, while Rachel battled with envy and discontentment as a result of difficulties conceiving a child with Jacob. Rachel and Leah's self-worth, self-identity, joy, and peace began to deteriorate, in turn creating bitterness toward God.

As the story continues, you'll later find out that God had a plan for each woman all along. No matter how much they compared themselves against the other, nothing could change the journey or destiny God put before them.

Sometimes we compare ourselves to other people. "I'm not as successful as her" or "I don't have what she has." We look at others and think, if only we had their jobs, possessions, life experiences, or talents then our lives would be better. In reality, those things won't make us more content with ourselves unless they align with God's plan for our lives.

God's will for your life was set before you were created. God isn't going to change the vision intended for you because you desire the life of someone else. So, when you find yourself falling into a pattern of comparison, focus on what makes you stand out from everyone else around you. Focus on what makes YOU unique!

REFLECTION

Write a list of 20 things that you love about yourself. I know it's sometimes difficult to highlight positive attributes about ourselves, so if you find yourself stuck, ask a close family member or friend. It may feel silly or uncomfortable, but those who love us the most often see wonderful things about us that we don't recognize.

Road to Discovery

SCRIPTURE

See what great love the Father has lavished on us, that we should be called children of God! And that is what we are! The reason the world does not know us is that it did not know him. *1 John 3:1 (NIV)*

DEVOTIONAL

We all have moments when we can't quite figure out who we are. This lack of awareness may make us feel like failures—like we are not good enough to advance in our careers or life, or that there's something wrong with us because we cannot communicate our desires or life goals. But what if we stopped trying to figure out who we are and instead tried to discover who God made us to be? Actor David A. R. White once said, "Life isn't always about finding yourself. More often than not, it's about discovering who God created you to be."[1]

Discovering our God-given identity is a lifelong journey. It's not something that happens in a snap, or with just one revelation. It's a process, and it takes time to get where you need to go. We will continue to grow and experience many different life transitions. No two seasons are the same, and each may require different versions of ourselves. But each season will require us to show up as God intended—as the version laid out in His blueprint.

Embrace this journey as you would any other adventure: with open arms and an open mind. Ask questions, seek answers, and trust that God is with you as you travel along this road of discovery. He is listening and waiting to reveal to us our identities for His will to be done here on Earth.

REFLECTION

Taking a journey to discover your God-given identity can be an exciting experience. But it can also be daunting, especially if you don't know where to start. Here are some tips for making the most of this self-discovery process:

♣ Make a plan for your journey. What questions do you want answered? What kind of information do you need? How will you track your progress? You may want to put together a checklist and then check off items as you complete them.

---

1 "A Quote from between Heaven and Hollywood," Goodreads, accessed September 18, 2023, https://www.goodreads.com/quotes/8290867-life-isn-t -always-about-finding-yourself-more-often-than-not, 16.

❧ Share your journey with someone who supports you. Ask them to pray for you and encourage you along the way—it's important to have someone who celebrates your progress and listens without judgment!

❧ Don't give up! Even if it doesn't go exactly how you planned, keep moving forward toward what God has called you to do in this world.

Sticks and Stones

SCRIPTURE

And now, dear brothers and sisters, one final thing. Fix your thoughts on what is true, and honorable, and right, and pure, and lovely, and admirable. Think about things that are excellent and worthy of praise. *Philippians 4:8 (NLT)*

DEVOTIONAL

What is one thing you were told as a child that as an adult you realize is a lie? I'll go first: "Sticks and stones may break my bones, but words will never hurt me."

Well, I hate to break it to you, but the lie detector test determined that is a LIE! Words hurt. Many of us, at some point in our lives, have experienced verbal abuse—be it name calling, bullying, or verbal intimidation. Whether it came from a sibling, school bully, or an authority figure whom we loved and trusted, I think we can agree we were hurt by those words. It's possible those experiences impacted our self-perception, self-reflection, and overall identity.

However, there is one form of verbal abuse we tend to forget and ignore, and that's negative self-talk. Too often, we are our worst critics and biggest bullies. So much so that we become oblivious of the mean and hurtful things we say about ourselves.

Now, don't get me wrong, I don't think anyone wakes up with a plan to tear themselves down with their own words. But negative self-talk can easily become our second language if we lack awareness and intentionality.

Think about a time when you were talking to a friend and said something along the lines of, "I hate the way my nose is shaped," "I will never be able to afford that car," "I'm not qualified enough for that promotion," or "I can't let go of grudges; that's just the way I am."

The power of our words impacts the ways in which we identify. Scripture tells us that life and death are in the power of the tongue (Proverbs 18:21)! We kill our self-perception and self-identity with the negativity we speak over ourselves. And yes, the way we perceive and speak to ourselves may be a direct result of the verbal abuse we have experienced in the past, but as adult women we now need to take ownership of our healing by training our minds to know and believe differently.

REFLECTION

Affirm what is uniquely amazing about you physically, mentally, spiritually, and professionally! Write down these affirmations on a piece of paper or index cards and put them where you will see them every day!

- ❀ I am a masterpiece, handcrafted by God's standard of beauty. I love the skin I am in.
- ❀ I have the power to create opportunities for love and success in my life.

🍀 I exude confidence and boldness in any room I enter.

🍀 Because I am called, I am qualified!

🍀 I matter!

🍀 God made no mistakes when He formed me. I love me, just as I am!

Intimacy Matters

SCRIPTURE

Abide in me, and I in you. As the branch cannot bear fruit by itself, unless it abides in the vine, neither can you, unless you abide in me. *John 15:4 (ESV)*

DEVOTIONAL

It's crazy to think that God is so detailed He knows the very number of hairs on our heads; something we could never know about ourselves. Not even our parents, spouses, children, or closest friends know us as intimately as God.

So, I think it's safe to say that developing a personal relationship with God is at the center of coming to know and embrace your true identity. Who knows the invention better than the inventor? Who knows the inner workings of the creation better than the creator? Who knows the child more personally than the one who's known her before she was placed in her mother's womb?

But building intimacy in a relationship is a two-way street. Just as God knows us, we must become acquainted with Him on a deeper level. In fact, throughout the Bible, God invites us to seek His face and be in relationship with Him.

It wasn't until I got past the cover of the Bible that I learned it wasn't about some universal dictator, but instead, a loving Father who wants to build intimacy with His children. We must look beyond the surface to discover the true essence of God and His character. From start to finish, the Bible helps guide us into the powerful presence of God so we can experience supernatural revelations—revelations about who He is and who He created us to be.

As Black women, discovering our God-given identity is essential to living our best lives and connecting with the divine. When we understand who we are in the eyes of God, we can begin to build a powerful and meaningful relationship with Him.

REFLECTION

There is no better way to build intimacy with God than through open, honest prayer. And there is no better place to encounter Him than in His creation, mother nature. This week, plan prayer time outdoors. Spend time having a prayerful exchange with the Father. Ask Him to reveal the true character of His nature as well as help you know your own.

Because of Them, We Can

SCRIPTURE

Let this be recorded for a generation to come, so that a people yet to be created may praise the Lord. *Psalm 102:18 (ESV)*

DEVOTIONAL

For centuries, Black women have endured being undervalued, under-protected, and underrepresented. Yet, we live, breathe, and walk in the ramifications of our ancestors who boldly embraced their uniqueness, culture, and God-given identity despite adversity.

Discovering our true identity unlocks pathways for generations after us to fulfill the destiny God has awaiting them. Our ancestors showed incredible courage and strength in paving the way for us to be successful. They passed down to us their spirit of hope and tenacity. We are all fortunate to stand upon the shoulders of their accomplishments, inspiring us to make the best of our lives and become the people we were destined to be.

They have been a pillar of strength and resilience through history, and their legacy continues to live on.

Now, think about someone who inspires you on your spiritual journey. Had that person not embraced their identity, which led to their purpose and calling, would you be where you are today? Our God is detailed, intentional, and meticulous about His plan, which is to spread the Good News and bring Him glory.

And guess what? You play a significant role in this plan! It's not by happenstance that you crossed paths with the person who inspires you. Nor is it happenstance that you are reading this devotional right now! You are as much a part of my assignment, which requires me to step fully into my God-given identity as the person who will benefit from you learning and embracing your identity. Think, circle of life.

Generations are settling in your womb, relying on you to embrace and stand firm on your God-given identity. Your walk with Christ isn't just about you! Embracing your God-given identity means that God's plan can be fulfilled. The others He has assigned to you can also reach their destinies and pave the way for the generations after them.

The torch has been passed, and each day we become our ancestors' wildest dreams. In an effort to honor those who came before us, may we have the courage to walk in their footsteps and create a more promising future for all by passing down a legacy of faith that is rooted in knowing who God called us to be.

REFLECTION

Leaving a legacy of faith is something we should all desire. Our future generations will benefit from the seeds we plant along our spiritual walk. Grab your journal and begin to write about what type of legacy you want to leave for future generations. What would you want them to know about Christ? What would you want them to know about the God-given identity of their lineage?

Becoming HER

SCRIPTURE

My old self has been crucified with Christ. It is no longer I who live, but Christ lives in me. So I live in this earthly body by trusting in the Son of God, who loved me and gave himself for me. *Galatians 2:20 (NLT)*

DEVOTIONAL

So, we've done the work to discover our God-given identity, but how do we nurture and develop our identity to be in alignment with our purpose and calling?

Who is she as a new being in Christ? What does God say about her? What does she believe about herself? What helps her remain on a continuum of spiritual growth and intact with her identity? How does she practice soul care to avoid spiritual burnout and becoming weary in her walk with Jesus? In what ways does the enemy try to distract and disrupt what she has come to know about herself? How is her identity a reflection of her purpose and calling?

As Black women, we are very strong and capable of accomplishing so much. But doing and being all the things makes it difficult to focus on getting to know ourselves and cultivating our relationship with our identity.

To unlock our potential and thrive in this world, we must become intentional and take time to explore and develop ourselves. That means carving out time to think and reflect on what makes us special and what drives us. Slow down and consider how you view the world and how the world views you.

When we tap into the unique qualities of our identity and explore them to the fullest, we unlock new levels of power, peace, and growth that help us reach our highest potential.

REFLECTION

It's time to build a relationship with who God has called you to be. Take the time to get to know her, love her, and celebrate her. Look over this list of ways in which you can nurture and develop your identity in Christ. Choose two activities from this list to incorporate into your routine starting TODAY!

- ♣ Practice Bible verse memorization. Find three scriptures that remind you of who God says you are, and memorize those.
- ♣ Create a space in your home for prayer and meditation. Meet God here and allow Him to reaffirm who you are.
- ♣ Fill a jar with affirmations celebrating who God called you to be. Whenever you need a reminder, visit your jar.
- ♣ Add a self-care day to your calendar every month. Rejuvenate your mind, body, soul, and spirit. Pay close attention to the things your physical and mental health respond to positively, and do more of that!

Liar, Liar

SCRIPTURE

Put on all of God's armor so that you will be able to stand firm against all strategies of the devil. *Ephesians 6:11 (NLT)*

DEVOTIONAL

You may have heard that the devil is a liar. And just in case you haven't, here is your notice: THE DEVIL IS A LIAR. *John 8:44 (ESV)*

Sometimes his lies are subtle and carry undertones of truth. Sometimes his lies are blatant, with no sugarcoating. No matter how he packages his lies, they are dangerous. If you don't know how to identify the false statements he is making to you, you may easily mistake his lies for the truth. These lies may present themselves as a lack of faith in God's Word, negative thoughts about self, and doubt in one's abilities, telling you that you are not who God has called you to be and cannot do what God has called you to do.

The enemy will go to great lengths to twist God's truth. He has a way of lying to us and stirring us from our innermost core, tearing away at the very foundation that lies beneath our true God-given identity. And even if we realize he's a liar, he'll tell more lies to destroy our sense of self. He knows that his lies aren't just meaningless. They can be self-defeating. Lies about who we are and what God says about us are especially destructive, because they lead to despair and disruption in the Kingdom of Christ.

What we believe about ourselves directly impacts how we show up for the Kingdom. Before God formed us in our mothers' wombs, he predestined an assignment to fulfill His greater purpose, an assignment that will be difficult to accomplish if we succumb to the lies of the enemy about who God handcrafted us to be. So, this means war. The stakes are high! Our purpose and calling are on the line.

We need to recognize when we are under attack so we can "put on the full armor of God" (Ephesians 6:11 [NIV]) and fight back. The Father prepared you for a war such as this and he tells us in John 8:31–32 (ESV): "If you abide in my word, you are truly my disciples, and you will know the truth, and the truth will set you free."

God will set you free from trickery of the devil with the truth of His Word.

REFLECTION

The enemy comes through with a vengeance. But we fight back harder. We can always stay one step ahead of his schemes if we are prepared for whatever he may present. This week, study Ephesians 6:10–18, The Armor of God. Meditate on which aspect of the armor you can build upon to give yourself better leverage when the enemy comes prowling.

Love the Skin You're In

SCRIPTURE

God paid a high price for you, so don't be enslaved by the world. *1 Corinthians 7:23 (NLT)*

DEVOTIONAL

Culture has a lot to say about who we should be and how we should look, think, feel, and act as Black women. According to culture, we should be strong, but soft. We should be independent, but dependent enough to not emasculate a man. We should be assertive in professional settings, but not too authoritative and risk being perceived as angry or aggressive. We should wear our natural hair, but keep it tamed in buns or ponytails.

How confusing is that? How confusing is it to have so many contraindications within the culture, not to mention the contraindications of what and who God says we are?

Culture is important to one's self-perception, self-image, and self-confidence. But as believers in Jesus Christ, we must be careful to not place culture on a pedestal where it has the ability to compromise our identity in Christ. As this week's scripture stated, Jesus bought us at a HIGH price. He shed His own blood and gave His life to call us His! We don't belong to our culture; we belong to Christ.

Black culture is freeing, soulful, and exudes pride. It represents our innermost exclusivity, while also forming a sense of connectedness to one another. Black is beautiful. The uniqueness that Black women bring to our culture and the world is astounding.

But before we are Black women, we are daughters of the Most High, commissioned to bring glory to God's Kingdom above all else! Our culture should enhance the uniqueness God has gifted us, not tear away at the identity He has assigned to us.

REFLECTION

Grab your journal and head to a quiet space. Now journal using the following prompt:

Is culture or the Word of God shaping my self-perception? In what ways? What cultural misconceptions can I get rid of to embrace my God-given identity?

Beauty Is Her Name

SCRIPTURE

Don't be concerned about the outward beauty of fancy hairstyles, expensive jewelry, or beautiful clothes. You should clothe yourselves instead with the beauty that comes from within, the unfading beauty of a gentle and quiet spirit, which is so precious to God. *1 Peter 3:3-4 (NLT)*

DEVOTIONAL

God is the ultimate beholder of beauty. He is the one who sees true beauty for what it's created to be. To Him, everything He creates is beautiful. Not because He did a stellar job of creating our facial structures or body types. Not because of our beautiful shades of Blackness, luscious lips, kinks, coils, braids, weaves, manicures, or creative fashion choices. Everything He creates is beautiful because He is the epitome of beauty. His very being embodies beauty.

Our true beauty comes from God and rests in our hearts. God gifts us with inner beauty at birth, and He never intends for anyone or anything to take it away. He wants us to walk in our beauty in every aspect of our lives, because He knows it equips us to walk boldly in His purpose for our lives, which is to love Him and others unconditionally and wholeheartedly.

Beauty has absolutely nothing to do with your outward appearance and everything to do with your hidden person, the person that no one sees at first glance. So, if asked, "What makes you beautiful?" how would you respond?

Are you kind, gentle, or generous? Do you love unconditionally, forgive easily, and steward well of what he has blessed you with? Do you prioritize your relationship with God, live righteously, and bring glory to His Kingdom?

As we align our identity with God, our inner beauty begins to permeate outward. When we begin to identify as children of God, we start to see more than just our outward appearance and what society deems as beautiful; we start to see ourselves as beautiful by God's design—by God's definition.

Our admission into our eternal resting place will not be dependent upon how well we apply our makeup or how creatively we style our hair. Our judgment day will not be marked by our physical beauty, but instead, we are judged by the beauty in our hearts.

REFLECTION

Say this prayer:

God,

Thank you for the gift of true inner beauty. Forgive me for being easily influenced by society's standards of outward beauty. Please help me to see and nurture the unfading beauty you placed inside of me, as I know that your love for me is immeasurable. Guide me to embrace the unique identity that you have given me, and to always walk in confidence knowing that I am fearfully and wonderfully made. May my inner beauty shine through and touch the lives of those around me.

Amen.

Did I Do That?

SCRIPTURE

Once again you will have compassion on us. You will trample our sins under your feet and throw them into the depths of the ocean! *Micah 7:19 (NLT)*

DEVOTIONAL

Mistakes are an inevitable part of life, and dare I say, necessary for growth and change. But Black women can easily feel pressured to get it right all the time. Society often gives us little room for error.

It becomes increasingly difficult to grow and move forward from our mistakes when we begin to formulate our identity around them. Identifying by our sins and mistakes—procrastinator, fornicator, addict, screw-up—does not align with who God says we are, which is forgiven, redeemed, and restored.

Sure, it's common to feel overwhelmed by our mistakes and sins, but it is completely unfair and unrealistic to take on the identity of our transgressions. Acknowledging we have challenges and struggles is one thing. Acknowledgment of our misdeeds and shortcomings leads us to repentance, which ultimately gives us leverage to walk in victory over them. But identifying with beliefs that God did not speak over us shatters our identity.

Black women, it is important to remember that our mistakes and challenges are a part of our journey of becoming, but they do not have to define who we are. Our true identity is found in Christ, who has called us His own. No matter what we have done or will do, you are loved and valued by Him. So do not let your mistakes hold you back. Instead, embrace the grace and forgiveness that comes with being a child of God. Walk confidently in your identity in Christ, and let that be your source of strength and confidence.

It's not God's intention for us to carry guilt, shame, or falsehoods. Instead, He offers forgiveness and grace to help us move forward and live a fulfilling life.

REFLECTION

It's time to rebrand ourselves as forgiven, redeemed, and restored. Here are four things you can do to overcome the guilt and shame associated with your sins and mistakes:

❖ Repent and forgive yourself. God requires that we confess our sins to Him but promises He will forgive us and make us clean again (1 John 1:9 [NLT]). Repenting gives us a fresh start to begin again. Acknowledging we made a mistake followed by forgiving ourselves frees us from self-persecution; thus, we can move forward on our journey.

❖ In all things, PRAY! Persistently pray for the deliverance from guilt and shame. Pray with intention and transparency, and allow God to show Himself faithful.

♣ Continue to show up for God no matter what! Despite the feelings of guilt and shame, do not allow these feelings to keep you from God because above all else, we still have a responsibility to the Kingdom.

♣ Affirm your identity in Christ. Remind yourself who God created you to be. Don't allow your mistakes to define you. God thinks so much more of you, and you need to know that!

Behold, a New You

SCRIPTURE

Throw off your old sinful nature and your former way of life, which is corrupted by lust and deception. Instead, let the Spirit renew your thoughts and attitudes. Put on your new nature, created to be like God—truly righteous and holy. *Ephesians 4:22–24 (NLT)*

DEVOTIONAL

The way we live our lives can speak volumes about who we think we are.

Have you ever wondered, "Am I truly a child of God?" But what does it mean to be a child of God? Am I expected to do things differently now? Is there something special I need to do that others don't need to do? What makes me different when I'm a child of God? How can others truly know that I am one of God's children? Can they really tell the difference? Can they see Him in my life?

Your identity isn't something you acquire from the outside world—it's God-ordained. Letting go of thoughts and behaviors that no longer align with your God-given identity is a powerful step toward living your best life. Releasing these negative patterns opens you up to positive growth and transformation. It may not always be easy, but by committing to the journey, you can find the strength to let go and embrace the truest version of yourself.

It's easy to get caught up in what you're used to, or even what you think you should be doing. But when we accept and declare God as our Lord and Savior, we become new creatures with a new lifestyle (2 Corinthians 5:17). Our old ways of living and thinking are renewed by God.

But this is not an automatic transformation. Embracing our new identity as children of God and a new lifestyle as Christian women will take intentionality, boundaries, prayer, and support from other believers. Our old ways of thinking and behaving no longer serve our new identity. Our environments, surroundings, habits, interpersonal relationships, and interactions will require change. Allowing God to align your thoughts and actions with your God-given identity is a powerful journey of growth and self-discovery. By surrendering to God's will, you can shed old habits and thought patterns that no longer serve you and begin to embrace new ways that honor your true self.

Think of the process as pouring new wine into a new wineskin. As Jesus taught his disciples, an old wineskin is no longer beneficial or capable of housing new wine. The old wineskin will burst, causing the wine to pour out and be ruined. The same goes for your new identity, which can no longer be housed in your old, worldly ways of being.

You have a purpose for which you were created, and no amount of pretending to be someone else will make it go away. You are not defined by the world around you or by your circumstances—you are defined by the one who created you and loves every part of your being.

REFLECTION

It's hard to let go of our old habits and ways of the world. But you are not in this world anymore. You are in Christ, which can feel scary. But there is nothing more comforting than knowing who you are and what your purpose is in life. So, take some time to reflect on how far you've come since becoming a disciple of Jesus Christ. Journal all the ways your life has changed since becoming a follower of Jesus Christ. What thought patterns have you been resistant to letting go? What ways of thinking and actions can you work on changing to align with your new identity?

Creature of Habit

SCRIPTURE

But they delight in the law of the Lord, meditating on it day and night. *Psalm 1:2 (NLT)*

DEVOTIONAL

Discovering your God-given identity as a Black woman can be an incredibly empowering experience. As you explore the stories and teachings in the Bible daily, you can gain insight into who God has made you to be. Through consistent prayer and reflection, you can build a relationship with God that will help you uncover the unique identity that He has given you.

These daily practices are the key to staying in alignment with your God-given identity. They also help you prioritize your relationship with God so that you can build intimacy and build up your spiritual muscle.

It's easy to begin our daily routines by checking our emails and social media accounts without acknowledging or realizing the impact it has on how we show up in the world. However, when our spiritual practices, like praying and reading our Word daily, are in the forefront of our daily routines, we easily focus on who we are and where we're going. Spiritual practices help us tap into our natural state so that we can live from a deeper level of spiritual consciousness. We will then begin to see change and transformation in every aspect of our lives, including our identity and its impact on the world around us.

This walk with Christ is not an act or a phase—it's a lifestyle that takes intentionality and commitment. As Christian women, we are called to live a life that honors God and reflects His image. The more intentional we are about our spiritual growth, the more we shine for Him! And it's in our daily habits that we start to become who God intended us to be.

REFLECTION

God wants us to spend time with Him every day because He knows that spending time with Him helps us to strengthen the foundation and discover our identity. It is then we can be confident in our purpose and walk boldly in our calling. Here are three tips to incorporate into your daily spiritual growth routine that is sure to reveal your God-given identity and build your connectedness to Christ.

1. Spend at least 15 minutes reading your Bible every day. Make it part of your routine, like brushing your teeth or getting dressed in the morning. You'll start seeing God's Word come alive in your life!

2. Find a quiet place where you can sit down with God and spend some quality time with Him each day. If there are other people around, try setting aside a few minutes to pray by yourself before joining them for dinner or whatever activity comes next on your schedule.

3. Get creative! Spending time with God doesn't have to be boring—find out what works best for YOU! There are tons of apps out there that can help you keep track of how much time you spend praying each day (and there are even more options if you don't have access to technology). Try something new.

The Me I See

SCRIPTURE

So do not throw away this confident trust in the Lord. Remember the great reward it brings you! *Hebrews 10:35 (ESV)*

DEVOTIONAL

It's easy to get caught up in the way people see us. But that doesn't mean those perceptions are true.

We are more than our circumstances, more than our past mistakes, and more than the opinions of others. We have been created by God with purpose and worth, and His love for us is greater than any other thing in this world or beyond it.

It's time for us to stop letting other people define us with their eyes or words or actions. It's time for us to become who we were meant to be—confident women who know our value and have no problem standing up for ourselves when someone tries to tear us down. It's time for us to stop hiding behind masks or letting other people tell us what we should look like or act like or say or do. We deserve better than that!

REFLECTION

Starting today—and every day after this one—we're going back out into the world with our heads held high, knowing that we are queens because God says so. Write these affirmations down on a sheet of paper and post them where you can see them every day. Take it one step further and send these affirmations to family and friends who need to hear this too. Post them to your social media to inspire and encourage another Black woman!

Affirmations:

You are a Black woman.

You are a daughter of the King.

You are made in His image and likeness.

You are a co-heir with Christ.

You have been blessed with all spiritual blessings in heavenly places.

You have been given the riches of Christ, and His inheritance is waiting for you in Heaven.

You are beautiful and intelligent, funny and kind, tenacious and strong. You are exactly who God created you to be, and He loves every single thing about your unique self.

You are a child of God, and He has given you an identity you can claim for yourself.

You are not a product of your environment.

You are more than a reflection of your family and friends.

Firm Foundation

SCRIPTURE

You didn't choose me. I chose you. I appointed you to go and produce lasting fruit, so that the Father will give you whatever you ask for, using my name. *John 15:16 (NLT)*

DEVOTIONAL

Sometimes, it's easy to lose sight of where you're headed—especially when you're in the midst of making decisions and dealing with life's everyday stressors, such as paying bills, household chores, and balancing multiple roles personally and professionally. But when you know who God has called you to be, it helps you stay en route toward fulfilling your purpose in this life, knowing that He has an amazing plan for you.

The key to fulfilling that purpose is knowing your identity as a daughter of God. Your identity is the foundation of everything that comes after it. The more solid your identity is, the better equipped you will be to pursue your purpose without being compromised during the process.

We owe it to ourselves to become in tune with who God called us to be. Our identity shapes our worldview and influences who we become. Without understanding who we are as Black women, we cannot truly understand our purpose in this world, our role as leaders in society, and our place in the Kingdom of God.

Your identity not only builds your confidence as a child of God but is the catalyst for fulfilling a very specific calling in your life. You are not here by accident—you have a mission, and it is unique to you. This requires you to be uniquely you!

God wants nothing more than for you to find your identity, because once you discover it, your purpose will become clear.

The Bible tells us that God created us in His own image (Genesis 1:27)—and He did so to fulfill His ultimate will and for us to live more abundantly.

REFLECTION

Understanding your identity is the foundation to walking in your unique, God-given purpose. Say this prayer:

Dear God,

Thank you for creating me in your image and giving me a unique identity and purpose. Help me to understand and embrace who I am, and to use my gifts and talents to serve you and others. Guide me in discovering and fulfilling my calling, and remind me that my worth and significance come from you alone. Thank you for your unconditional love and grace and for the opportunity to be a part of your Kingdom work.

In Jesus's name,

Amen.

Part 2

Purpose

Purpose-Full

SCRIPTURE

Furthermore, because we are united with Christ, we have received an inheritance from God, for he chose us in advance, and he makes everything work out according to his plan. *Ephesians 1:11 (NLT)*

DEVOTIONAL

You may have heard someone say they found their purpose or discovered what they were meant to do. But what does that mean?

Well, the Bible tells us in Ephesians 2:10 that "we are God's workmanship, created in Christ Jesus for good works, which God prepared beforehand, that we should walk in them." The word "prepared" means that God already arranged our life's purpose before we were born into this world. And these plans are not just ordinary plans but extraordinary ones. Plans that He intends to use to spread the gospel and build His Kingdom.

God does not want us to be robots that perform functions without purpose or direction. He wants us to have a purpose and a destiny, so that He may use us for His glory.

We, as Black women, come in different colors, shapes, sizes, and personalities. Each of us has been uniquely created with a specific talent or gift that makes us unique. But we all share one thing in common: God has given each of our lives a purpose! Maybe He's given you the gift of leadership to start a ministry that tackles homelessness in your community. Or maybe you have been gifted with a beautiful singing voice that helps usher believers into a deep space of worship. Or maybe you have the gift of encouragement and are called to encourage at-risk youth toward a path of righteousness.

Whatever your gift and whatever His purpose, God knows who He created us to be. He knows what strengths we have and what talents we possess as His daughters. Most importantly, He knows how he wants us to utilize those strengths in His Kingdom, for His glory.

REFLECTION

As you prepare to explore God's purpose for your life, write a letter of encouragement to your future self. Detail what you have made it through to get to this point in your walk with Christ. Tell her your expectations and fears as it relates to your God-ordained purpose.

The Blueprint

SCRIPTURE

God has now revealed to us his mysterious will regarding Christ—which is to fulfill his own good plan. And this is the plan: At the right time he will bring everything together under the authority of Christ—everything in heaven and on earth. *Ephesians 1: 9–10 (NLT)*

DEVOTIONAL

Before anything can be built, one must have a blueprint. A blueprint is essential to the planning and building phase as it ensures success of the intended outcome.

Before creating the world and everything in it, God had a plan. Light and darkness, land and water, man and woman, even Jesus Christ all served a purpose and was a part of God's intentionality and well-orchestrated plan to bring glory to Himself.

We too are a part of God's blueprint to establish His Kingdom here on Earth. Our life's purpose stems from God's ultimate plan for us to love Him, love others, and share the good news, that it may spread throughout all nations.

We are commissioned to use our unique talents and gifts to serve within the Kingdom to share the goodness of God in the hearts of men, women, and children everywhere we go.

Our journeys may be individually unique. And we each may serve a different purpose in different capacities, but if each of us serves our purpose with our whole heart, we will ensure God's plan comes to pass. *We are a part of the blueprint!*

We are Kingdom ambassadors who represent God in every aspect of our lives—including our jobs, families, communities, and schools. No matter our respective assignments, callings, roles, titles, or positions, the glory of God should be the motivation behind why and how we walk boldly in our purpose on Earth. We are essential to God's blueprint for the Kingdom. Building the kingdom is a group project among believers that requires us to all do our parts.

Without your voice and your actions, this Kingdom of God would be missing a vital function of the plan. And although we do not have the power to derail God's ultimate plan by not walking in our purpose, we can live a more empowered and fulfilled life when we are in position to do exactly what He's called us to.

REFLECTION

God has given us a unique purpose to bring glory to Him. It is our responsibility to build His Kingdom by reaching out to others in love and sharing the gospel.

We can do this by:

- ❧ Loving God with all our heart, soul, mind, and strength.
- ❧ Loving our neighbors as ourselves.
- ❧ Sharing the good news of Jesus Christ.
- ❧ Worshiping God through prayer, praise, and fellowship.

Of the four listed above, which of these can you do more of to build God's Kingdom? Now, write a list of three ways you can begin incorporating your selection into your daily routine.

Seek and Find

SCRIPTURE

The purpose in a man's heart is like deep water, but a man of understanding will draw it out. *Proverbs 20:5 (ESV)*

DEVOTIONAL

The question of purpose is an intriguing one because it's not something we can simply figure out by looking at our lives. It's something that must be discovered through the course of our journey with God. A journey that is individualized.

We don't pick our purpose, but instead, we partner with God to uncover it. But sometimes it feels like there are too many demands on our time, too many responsibilities that pull us in different directions. It seems impossible to find time for ourselves—to be able to spend some time with God and get a sense of what His plan is for us personally. But when we are intentional about discovering our calling and connecting with God, our purpose become clearer.

It is important for Black women to understand that purpose isn't something that we earn or choose—it's something God assigned to us before we came into this world (Jeremiah 1:4 [NLT]).

Discovering our purpose is a process. Praying and asking God to reveal His will for our lives is an important part of that process. By doing so, we not only acknowledge that our purpose is not our own but create space for God to reveal His perfect will for our life.

When we prioritize the discovery of our God-given purpose, we're able to do the things that we love without having to force ourselves. We're able to live a life that is not defined by the standards of society or man. We'll be able to serve God and others in ways that only we can, using the Black Girl Magic that's woven directly into the fabric of our being!

REFLECTION

Revelations are received as we build intimacy with God through prayer. Prayer helps to prepare our hearts and minds for the things God needs us to know to complete His good and perfect will. Read, recite, and write the prayer below. But remember, communication is a two-way street, so take time to sit and listen to how God responds to your prayer.

Say this prayer:

Heavenly Father, the creator of all purpose and mastermind behind all things that are good. Today I surrender my plans to you. I only want the purpose you have set out for me. Help me to replace the fleshly desires of my heart with passion for your plans that, according to your Word, will ultimately prevail. Forgive me for seeking purpose without you. Today and forever, I welcome your divine direction, instruction, and will for my life. May my purpose be saturated with your wisdom, your knowledge, and your ways so that your Kingdom will reign throughout all of Earth.

The Perfect Gift

SCRIPTURE

Whatever is good and perfect is a gift coming down to us from God our Father, who created all the lights in the heavens. He never changes or casts a shifting shadow. *James 1:17 (NLT)*

DEVOTIONAL

Doesn't it feel good when someone gives you a gift that you have long desired? What about a gift that you didn't even know you needed but turns out to be beneficial to you and those around you? Did you feel joy? Peace? Did it improve your life in any way?

Knowledge of our God-ordained purpose is just that—a gift! Many of us have longed to discover it. Some of us never even considered that our purpose would be what it is. It was shocking and surprising... but still very much fulfilling.

The gift of knowing our purpose is such a special one because that is God's way of showing us that He trusts us with His vision for our life. Knowing our purpose is a huge responsibility. There are souls attached to our purpose.

It's a part of God's plan. Someone, somewhere is depending on us to discover and live out our God-given purpose. Someone's salvation is dependent upon you birthing that ministry, writing that book, sharing your testimony and encouraging words, getting that degree, or becoming that leader in the community.

Many wander the Earth having not yet discovered their purpose because they have not shown trustworthiness with such revelation.

When God withholds the disclosure of our purpose, it is more often than not a result of not being in position or mature enough to receive such a gift. Think about it—a CEO can't give us a promotion if we're not performing in our current role. A mother wouldn't give her toddler keys to drive her car.

God is a good, good father. He knows us better than we know ourselves. He knows our capabilities, our strengths, and areas of needed development. His divine omniscience qualifies Him to promote us to the next level in our walk because He knows our hearts, our thoughts, and our readiness to receive such a blessing.

REFLECTION

Preparing for the things that we are expecting from God puts us in a better position to receive and sustain what He gives us, when He gives it to us.

Reflect on one thing you can do to prepare for stewardship of your purpose. Start doing that thing TODAY! Do not wait! The time is NOW!

God-fident Prayers

SCRIPTURE

So we have not stopped praying for you since we first heard about you. We ask God to give you complete knowledge of his will and to give you spiritual wisdom and understanding. Then the way you live will always honor and please the Lord, and your lives will produce every kind of good fruit. All the while, you will grow as you learn to know God better and better. *Colossians 1:9–10 (NLT)*

DEVOTIONAL

There's something about that lightbulb moment of discovering your purpose that makes you feel invincible!

Unlocking that level of clarity propels our spiritual journey to new heights! We become free from the bondage of purposelessness and enter into a world of meaningful awakening. But how do we know if what we have identified as our purpose is in alignment with the Lord's will for our life? How do we know this is not a self-appointed calling?

Wouldn't it be ideal for God to descend from the Heavens to give us a direct yes or no? But how many of us would take our answer, run with it, and never look back? God is intentional by creating a means to which we would have to seek His face to discover the reason behind our existence. Having knowledge of God's will for our lives requires building an intimate relationship with Him and having complete dependency on His sovereign leadership. By doing so, you will not only gain spiritual wisdom but learn to recognize His voice and direction.

This week's scripture gives us somewhat of a guide to help determine if our purpose is God ordained. Does our purpose honor and please God? Does our purpose produce good fruit? Are we growing spiritually as a result of living out our purpose?

What we often call "the little voice in the back of our heads" or a "gut feeling" is most likely the gentle push of the Holy Spirit leading us down a path paved by The Author of our story.

Growing in our faith increases our discernment. It does not get any more magical for Black women than to walk God-fidently in the purpose you know He predestined just for you!

REFLECTION

Having discernment takes spiritual fitness. It's like a spiritual muscle that must be worked out in a routine saturated in spiritual discipline and consistency. By spending time with God through prayer and in his Word daily, we'll begin to recognize the gentleness of His voice. So, let's practice. Take 10 minutes each day of this week meditating on this week's scripture, praying for God's wisdom to download into your spirit, and sitting in silence to hear His response. Record what you hear from God in a journal or notebook.

Equipped for Purpose

SCRIPTURE

Our God gives you everything you need, makes you everything you're to be. *2 Thessalonians 1:2 (MSG)*

DEVOTIONAL

It's pretty typical of God to call us to something that we otherwise deem ourselves unqualified for. Whether it's because of a lack of knowledge or outright fear, we often disqualify ourselves from the purpose God destined for our lives.

And that's okay.

Many of our most notable biblical heroes felt inadequate for the purpose God placed before them. Sarah felt she was too old to become pregnant and birth a child. Moses felt his speech impediment would hinder his effectiveness as a leader. And we can only begin to imagine what Mary felt, as an unwedded teenager, charged with birthing and raising the Messiah.

So, that seemingly unobtainable purpose assigned to us is just God's modus operandi (MO). He makes no mistakes. His objective is not to assign us with a purpose that makes us feel comfortable. But, instead, He develops our trust and dependence on Him through extraordinary callings. He qualifies us with every skill and resource needed to fulfill His good and perfect plan—despite our fears, doubts, and feelings of inadequacy. Because remember, our purpose isn't about what makes us feel good or happy, it's about bringing glory to our matchless, merciful Father.

So, yes, it's okay for us to not FEEL equipped for our purpose—we're human. But what's not okay is allowing our feelings of inadequacy to impede our pursuit of purpose. We must KNOW that we are equipped!

Acknowledge your feelings but remind yourself that *If He calls you to it, He'll see you through it*!

REFLECTION

It's hard for many of us to imagine ourselves capable of fulfilling such a significant role in God's master plan. However, we must remember that He is the author of the beginning and the end. He not only knows what we are capable of (because He has walked this path before us), He also created us for His specific purpose in this specific time.

Having trust in God despite your human emotions requires a complete shift in mindset. Say these affirmations as you begin to train your mind to know that YOU, BLACK QUEEN, ARE EQUIPPED!

Affirmations:

I am equipped to prosper in every good work.

Because God is reliable, I lack no good thing.

God's Word equips me to walk righteously in my purpose.

No matter what obstacle I face, I will remain steadfast in pursuit of the God-given purpose for my life.

Resources flow to me in abundance.

Make No Mistake

SCRIPTURE

And we know that for those who love God all things work together for good, for those who are called according to his purpose. *Romans 8:28 (ESV)*

DEVOTIONAL

Want to know a secret? God will take our mistakes and use them for His purpose!

Listen, we give ourselves way too much credit when we make mistakes. We do not have the power to thwart God's plan or purposes. Nothing we can do will derail what God has already brought to completion. We are born sinners. And as born-again Christians, the goal is to live righteously, not perfectly.

Want to know another secret?

God knows we're not perfect, and He doesn't expect us to be. Like any parent who knows what mishap their toddler is about to make before they make it, God knows His children. He knows our patterns, our habits, and our ways. He knows our deepest temptations, strongholds, and the sins we have difficulty parting from. Nothing we can ever do will surprise God.

Yes, He holds us to a standard of righteous living, but not perfection. It's impossible for us to be perfect and completely free from sin, which is why He sent his son, Jesus Christ, to Calvary. We will mess up. We will make mistakes. We all fall short of the glory of our Father.

But our God is a gracious God. Romans 8:28 tells us that God works all things together for the good of those who love Him. He will use your greatest victories, and even greater mishaps, to see His plan come to pass. So, do not beat yourself up for making a mistake. But instead, acknowledge your error, repent, learn from it, and push forward in Jesus's name.

REFLECTION

Mistakes are necessary in life. They not only serve as an avenue for learning and growth on our own spiritual journey but become a part of our testimony, which can bless others on theirs. Sharing our testimony with someone else can help them get to know God as a forgiving, gracious, merciful Father.

As Black Christian women, we have the responsibility to encourage our sisters who are also on this walk with Christ. So, journal about a time God used a mistake for your good. How can your testimony help another Black woman in your life?

Prepared On Purpose

SCRIPTURE

"For I know the plans I have for you," declares the LORD, "plans to prosper you and not to harm you, plans to give you hope and a future." *Jeremiah 29:11 (NLT)*

DEVOTIONAL

We are not meant to live life without purpose. We may not know what it is yet, but we can be sure that God knows, and He has a plan for us. He has always known your purpose and has been preparing you for it since birth.

The people, places, and things in our past are all building blocks on the path toward our future. We have gained wisdom, knowledge, and experience by living through it all. Our stories have added value to the world because of everything that has happened up until this point in time.

Imagine being labeled as "talkative" as a young child but growing to become a motivational speaker. Maybe God instructed you to move to a new city where you didn't know anyone but met the very person who helped you to fund your dream business. Or the heartbreak you experienced as a young adult that made room for you to pursue a deep, intimate relationship with God. These are all common life experiences that we may not realize was God preparing us for our destiny.

God is the ultimate planner, and if we take the time to truly reflect on our past, we're guaranteed to see His handprint in every season. He has prepared us for our purpose all the while.

Black women's unique life experiences shape who we are today. We've faced challenges and overcome obstacles that have made us smarter, stronger, and better equipped for the work God has called upon us. When we acknowledge this gift and use it to our advantage, we become agents of change in the Kingdom.

We can't always see the big picture because we don't know what's coming next or where it will lead us. But when we trust in Him as a Shepherd, who intimately knows his sheep, we can follow blindly knowing that we are in the hands of the one who ever so graciously tends to us, guides us, and protects His flock.

There's no other person on Earth who can bring to the world what God has designed for you!

REFLECTION

God is not a God of confusion, but He is a God of peace and order. He wants to give you peace about your future by giving you direction and purpose in life.

Pray this prayer:

Our good and faithful Shepherd, help me to accept your good and perfect plan. Remove any negative feeling associated with the things of my past, for I now know they were intentional for the purpose you have assigned me. Help me to focus on the lessons and not losses of my life experiences and move forward with a heart postured for trust in you. In Jesus's name, amen.

Not So Fast!

SCRIPTURE

In his grace, God has given us different gifts for doing certain things well. So, if God has given you the ability to prophesy, speak out with as much faith as God has given you. If your gift is serving others, serve them well. If you are a teacher, teach well. If your gift is to encourage others, be encouraging. If it is giving, give generously. If God has given you leadership ability, take the responsibility seriously. And if you have a gift for showing kindness to others, do it gladly. *Romans 12:6-8 (NLT)*

DEVOTIONAL

Developing your spiritual gifts is a process. It's a journey of discovery, growth, and development.

When we are children, our parents help us to develop our skills and talents by offering words of encouragement (or criticism). As adults, we learn from experience—whether it's through trial and error or failure after failure (which can sometimes take years). And then there are those rare individuals with natural abilities who did not have to work as hard at developing them.

No matter the category you fall in, we all have the responsibility of growing and developing in our purpose. We should never stop being students of our purpose.

Discovering our purpose is exciting and is a milestone on our walk with Christ. However, we can become so excited that we jump the gun and begin performing without proper preparation. An underdeveloped purpose can cause delay and detriment, rather than progression and production of fruit.

Let's consider Jesus's preparation process for example. Jesus's purpose was appointed before He came to this world. Although there is not much detail about Jesus's upbringing, we can assume that it played an intricate part in Jesus fulfilling his God-ordained purpose later in life.

At age twelve, we see Jesus mingling with elders of the temple, asking questions, and soaking up knowledge about the gospel. When Mary prompted Jesus to come home, He began pleading with his parents because He felt He was ready to begin fulfilling His purpose. However, it was not yet time.

By age 33, Jesus was baptized and began walking out the purpose God intended for Him while on Earth, but only after many years of seeking, studying, and preparing. Imagine if Jesus's parents had allowed Him to remain in the temple at 12 years old. Would the purpose have prevailed in the way it was intended?

It just wasn't time. There was still more knowledge, skills, wisdom, and maturity needed. And this is not to be confused with perfectionism but, rather, trusting the process and becoming well equipped.

REFLECTION

We can learn so much from Jesus and the development of His purpose. Although Jesus and those closest to Him knew of His purpose, it took time to learn, grow, and develop to bring His purpose to full capacity. We see Jesus study, ask questions of wise leaders, accept righteous judgment and wise counsel from His parents about timing, and submit to being baptized by John the Baptist—all before walking fully in His purpose.

Write down three ways you can develop your purpose with the help of those closest to you, your church, and local community.

1. ....

....

....

....

....

2. ....

....

....

....

....

3. ....

....

....

....

....

What's Your Influence?

SCRIPTURE

You are the salt of the earth. But what good is salt if it has lost its flavor? Can you make it salty again? It will be thrown out and trampled underfoot as worthless. You are the light of the world—like a city on a hilltop that cannot be hidden. No one lights a lamp and then puts it under a basket. Instead, a lamp is placed on a stand, where it gives light to everyone in the house. In the same way, let your good deeds shine out for all to see, so that everyone will praise your heavenly Father. *Matthew 5:13–16 (NLT)*

DEVOTIONAL

Since we live in the days of social media, we should all be pretty familiar with the term "influencer." No matter which platform you subscribe to or how much time you spend scrolling, you are sure to come across someone who tries to sell you a product, service, or investment in some sort of lifestyle.

As believers in Jesus Christ, we are called to be influencers for the Kingdom. But instead of the purchase of products or services, God charges us to promote a life of freedom and service to the Kingdom.

Like salt and light, we are to preserve what is good and holy and illuminate where darkness exists in the world. God created Black women to be leaders who live a life of significance, impact, and influence. We are the hands and feet of Jesus, sharing His good works. We are to represent who He is and what He stands for in the ways we engage, love, and serve others.

When we look at the world around us, it's easy to feel like we're small and insignificant. But the truth is that each of us holds a special place in God's heart and a particular purpose in His Kingdom.

The Bible highlights the stories of inspirational women such as Deborah and Esther, who were divinely selected to guide their communities with strength and wisdom, bringing glory to God. The legacy of Black women leaders is a testament to the authority God gives us to take charge in our families, churches, communities, and the world!

By leading with humility, compassion, and integrity, we can inspire and guide others toward a deeper relationship with God. Let us embrace our calling as leaders and strive to make a positive impact in the lives of those around us.

REFLECTION

As Christians, we have an amazing opportunity to be a part of something bigger than ourselves. God has called us to serve Him and help others do the same. Reflect on this week's scripture and think about how you will show up as the salt and light of the world in your home, workplace, church, and community. Share your thoughts and plans with someone you trust to hold you accountable. Schedule a time this week to check in with the person you identified and share your progress.

Community Project

SCRIPTURE

Just as our bodies have many parts and each part has a special function, so it is with Christ's body. We are many parts of one body, and we all belong to each other. *Romans 12: 4–5 (NLT)*

DEVOTIONAL

"Two heads are better than one."

"Iron sharpens iron."

"If you want to go fast, go alone; if you want to go far, go together."

We have all heard one, if not all, of the scriptures, quotes, and sayings above. And they are all true. God did not intend for us to do life alone, and that includes discovering and fulfilling our life's purpose.

Community plays a significant role in our growth and development as believers. It is within community you encounter like-mindedness and accountability (which are imperative for our obedience to follow God's will for our lives).

Not to mention, after we accept and profess Jesus as our Lord and Savior, we become a part of the body of Christ. A body, just like our own, functions best when its individual parts work together as a collective to accomplish goals—to breathe, live, and grow.

We are all designed to provide a specific function within the body of Christ to fulfill God's plan. When we are not in place fulfilling our purpose, the body has a missing piece—an extremely valuable piece.

Despite the media's narrative that Black women cannot band together to make a difference, building a community grounded in unity and love among us *all* can do wonders for the Kingdom.

REFLECTION

God created the concept of community to help us discover and fulfill our purpose together. Through our relationships, we can grow in our faith, receive support, and use our unique gifts to serve God and others. As we come together in community, we are strengthened and empowered to live out our calling and make a positive impact in the world.

In your journal, describe who's in your current community. What Kingdom assignments do you all work on together? How can you bring more unity, love, and cohesiveness to your community?

If you are not in a Christ-centered community and find yourself doing life alone, I encourage you to seek out a community this week. If not within your local church or where you live, research online Christian communities and join one. We cannot walk this walk alone! God never intended it to be that way.

Multipurpose Queen

SCRIPTURE

To everything there is a season, a time for every purpose under heaven. *Ecclesiastes 3:1 (NKJV)*

DEVOTIONAL

When we think of our life's purpose, we may believe it means a single mission. However, we have several purposes to which God may call us throughout our lifetime.

We all play different roles and have multiple titles that may require various talents, skills, and versions of ourselves. Therefore, we serve several purposes.

Our purpose can change depending upon the season of life we are in or the situations we encounter. We may serve a different purpose in motherhood than we do in our career. We may be called to serve two different purposes in two different ministries at church. Our purpose in our twenties may change, grow, and expand in our thirties.

Furthermore, our purpose consists of more than grand achievements. It also includes the small gestures of kindness and love that we extend to others. Every smile, every word of encouragement, every act of compassion that is orchestrated by God can have a profound impact on someone's life.

Every time we help someone in need, we're fulfilling a purpose. Every time we make someone laugh, we're fulfilling a purpose. Every time we do something kind for no other reason than to show someone love, we're fulfilling a purpose. By embracing both the big and small moments of life, we can discover a sense of purpose that transcends our individual accomplishments and connects us to something greater than ourselves.

REFLECTION

Each day we rise with breath in our lungs and blood running through our veins, we have a purpose to fulfill. For anyone who may be dealing with feelings of purposelessness or is on a journey to discover their purpose, remember to not discount the small, everyday purposes God assigns you. At the end of each day this week, spend 5 to 10 minutes writing down how God used you that day. Think of how you helped someone, made someone smile, or shared the love of Christ via your words or actions. Whether small or grand, may we never underestimate our power to make a difference in the Kingdom.

Our Purpose, His Plans

SCRIPTURE

Many are the plans in a person's heart, but it is the LORD's purpose that prevails. *Proverbs 19:21 (NIV)*

DEVOTIONAL

There's a great deal of pressure on Black women to be "successful," and we try to measure our success in many ways: by the amount of money we make, if people recognize our achievements, or how happy we are with ourselves. But none of these things will ever truly satisfy us, because they aren't what God wants for us!

From an early age we're told that without a plan for success we will fail. We are asked "What do you want to be when you grow up?" as children, encouraged to create vision boards, and prompted to write out five (sometimes ten) year plans. There is nothing wrong with having a plan for our lives, but there is an issue when we fail to include God in the planning stage. We often leave no room for His vision, plans, or will when we set out to obtain success.

Now, plans are important, as they provide order, organization, and structure. However, when we understand that God's plan will prevail, we'll approach the process differently. Our measures of success are then in alignment with what brings glory to God.

Success to Him looks like obeying His word, healing traumas, and overcoming sin—all while loving and serving Him wholeheartedly. Our purpose is going to always be rooted in heavenly magnitudes of success.

God is not concerned about our plaques or certificates, our promotions or bank accounts. He cares nothing about the plans we have for ourselves. He wants us to know Him, love Him, and serve Him. When we do this—when we put Him first in our lives—we find that our purpose comes more easily.

REFLECTION

We must be careful not to be deceived by the visuals of a luxurious life, assuming that materialistic wealth, as defined by society, equals purpose or success.

Say this prayer:

Lord, our purpose-giver and omniscient ruler, please help me to focus on your purpose for my life and to trust in your plan for my success. Father, please transform my mind to view purpose and success for what you have created them to be and not as society defines them. Remove the sinful nature of greed and desire for purposeless wealth from my heart. God, I welcome you on this journey to identifying and developing the purpose you have assigned to me. May you receive all glory from my obedience as I boldly and confidently walk in the purpose you have set before me!

Serve a Purpose

SCRIPTURE

"The Son of Man came not to be served but to serve, and to give his life as a ransom for many." *Mark 10:45 (ESV)*

DEVOTIONAL

In Matthew 6, Jesus teaches us how to pray. He tells us that we should pray for God's will to be done on Earth as it is in Heaven. But what does this mean?

God desires for the Earth to be free of sin, full of love, and for His name to be glorified. It's His will that the world operates in the same ways as the Kingdom of Heaven.

As believers, we have to not only pray and believe our prayers will come to pass, we must also take action. One way we do this is by humbly serving one another. Serving others is a vital part of God's will for our lives. We are called to serve because it is our purpose to glorify God. God wants us to yield to His will, rather than our own, for the purpose of building up His church and His people.

When we serve others with love, kindness, and generosity, we represent the true heart of God. We walk in our life's purposes, becoming better, stronger warriors of Christ. Our faith runs deeper and so does our relationship with Jesus Christ. Additionally, serving others strengthens our own character development. We need to look beyond ourselves so that we can help others find positive influences in their lives and bring them closer to Christ.

Serving others can give our lives a deeper sense of purpose. Devoting ourselves to service allows us to align our actions with what God values and cultivate a sense of purpose that transcends our individual needs and desires. The Bible is full of stories of people who were willing to sacrifice their lives for God's Kingdom. Jesus is one of these examples. His time on Earth was spent healing, feeding, and serving others.

We are also ambassadors for God. When we focus on helping and supporting those around us, we not only make a positive impact on their lives, but we also find fulfillment in our own.

REFLECTION

If you have not yet discovered your purpose, serving is a great way to discover where best you serve in the Kingdom. If you have discovered your purpose, then serving others is an excellent way to hone and develop your skills. Just imagine the outcome—a community of Black women combining our Black Girl Magic to serve one another and our communities.

This week, study John 13:12–17. Take note of Jesus's example and heart posture as a servant leader. Using His example of servanthood, reflect on how you can be more like Jesus as you serve others.

Get Thee Behind Me

SCRIPTURE

But your iniquities have made a separation between you and your God, and your sins have hidden his face from you so that he does not hear. *Isaiah 59:2 (ESV)*

DEVOTIONAL

Nothing is worse than working so hard for something, just to feel like one bad decision takes it all away. That's what it can sometimes feel like when we are in the pursuit of purpose but become bound by sin.

By nature, we are all sinful creatures. God does not expect for us to be sinless people because we are incapable of perfection. However, as believers, we are charged with resisting sin at all costs and to repent when we do fall victim. Sin and purpose cannot coexist. Sin is a barrier between you and God's will for your life. When we sin against God, our relationship with Him becomes tainted. When we fail to pursue righteousness, we no longer operate in the will of God.

Although scripture tells us that nothing can separate us from the love of God, it's in our human nature to feel distant from God when we sin. Like a wedge has come between us. Once our relationship with God becomes strained, it is extremely difficult to receive directions regarding the next steps in our purpose. When we sin and don't repent, we allow it to control our lives instead of God.

But, when we consciously obey the Word of God, we are saying "no" to the things that dishonor Him and "yes" to a purposeful life.

REFLECTION

Sin is an enemy that has invaded our lives and must be resisted. If you are struggling with sin in any area of your life, then I encourage you to repent and seek God's forgiveness so He can help you overcome it. The prophet Isaiah said, "Wash yourselves; make yourselves clean; remove the evil of your deeds from my sight." (Isaiah 1:16) Even though he was speaking specifically to Israel at this time, his words apply to all of us today as well. We need to be cleansed from our sins and made new in Him so that we can fulfill His purpose for our lives.

Grab your journal and write a prayer of repentance. Be specific and list all the ways you have sinned again God. Ask for God's forgiveness and help to turn you away from sin.

Doubt Doesn't Live Here Anymore

SCRIPTURE

Trust in the LORD with all your heart; do not depend on your own understanding. Seek his will in all you do, and he will show you which path to take. *Proverbs 3:5–6 (NLT)*

DEVOTIONAL

It's difficult to have confidence in something we cannot see. Scripture tells us that God has plans for us that do not include failure or disaster (Jeramiah 29:11); however, when there is an unexpected change in circumstances, a tragedy strikes, or someone shares their skepticism about our path, it becomes increasingly difficult to trust the Lord's plans.

It's not like we can just call Him on the phone and get a direct answer on whether or not we are walking down the right path. All we have is trust.

But if we remain diligent in our prayer life and reading of the Word, trust is all we will need. Walking confidently with God requires blind faith. But the enemy will try any tactic he can to make us doubt what we have come to know as true; and that is God is faithful, consistent, all-knowing, and has plans to provide us with a prosperous, peaceful life.

Doubt is the killer of purpose. And it's the easiest way for the enemy to obstruct pursuit of our God-given purpose. Instead of looking to the Lord and trusting His Word, we will begin to seek confirmation and validation from the world. Or even worse, we will totally neglect our purpose for complacency and comfortability, because uncertainty is just too much to bear.

We cannot afford to allow ourselves to be discouraged by the schemes of the enemy to make us doubt our purpose. Even family or friends may not understand because they do not know the value we add to God's Kingdom. Instead, we must stay focused on our divine calling and always remember that there is no person or circumstance that can stop us from fulfilling our destinies!

REFLECTION

We must not allow the whispers of the enemy to influence our actions or beliefs. We must trust in the plans of the Lord. Even when things don't go as planned and others try to doubt our purpose, we must not lean on our own understanding. Nor should we convince ourselves that we are not capable, qualified, or handcrafted to fulfill the purpose God has bestowed.

Affirmations:

I trust God because He is the author of my life's story.
I never experience losses, only lessons!
I walk in faith and trust in God's plans for me.

I am worthy of the best God has to offer!

Because God is working everything for my good, every trial is an opportunity for me to learn and grow.

Empty Frame

SCRIPTURE

As Jesus and the disciples continued on their way to Jerusalem, they came to a certain village where a woman named Martha welcomed Him into her home. Her sister, Mary, sat at the Lord's feet, listening to what He taught. But Martha was distracted by the big dinner she was preparing. She came to Jesus and said, "Lord, doesn't it seem unfair to you that my sister just sits here while I do all the work? Tell her to come and help me." But the Lord said to her, "My dear Martha, you are worried and upset over all these details! There is only one thing worth being concerned about. Mary has discovered it, and it will not be taken away from her." *Luke 10: 38–42 (NLT)*

DEVOTIONAL

What happens on our journey with Christ when what we are doing becomes more important than why we are doing it? Our purpose begins to drift slowly away from us.

If we're honest, when we operate in the Black Girl Magic God blessed us with, it has the ability to stretch us with responsibilities and opportunities that require much of our focus and attention. Though, we can become easily distracted by our fears, tasks, or obtaining worldly success.

When we become distracted by anything other than our purpose—our "why"—God loses the glory, and instead, our distractions are glorified. On top of that, our alignment with God is shaken and we lose focus on the reason for our existence and calling.

This is the trick of the enemy.

The enemy wants us to forget about what God has in store for us. He tries to convince us that pursuing our purpose isn't worth it or that something else requires more of our attention and focus. Simple! It is the enemy's goal to disrupt God's plan. We must make it difficult for him to gain the victory over us. God has given us the victory, but we still have to fight against the schemes of the enemy by avoiding distractions at all costs.

Our purpose on Earth is to know, serve, and tell others about God. When you know your purpose, you will say goodbye to all the distractions that try to steal your mind, heart, and attention away from Him.

So, do not get distracted by the work! Do not get distracted by the trials that may arise! Do not get distracted by the accolades and accomplishments! Stay seated at the feet of Jesus and seek His face daily in all the things we do. Don't become so enticed by the frame that you miss the bigger picture. A frame serves no purpose if there's nothing to fill it.

REFLECTION

As Christian women, we must avoid the distractions of the enemy while pursuing our purpose. We must also be alert and aware as there are some things that may seem innocent, but they will pull us away from our destiny.

Grab your journal and a pen. Write down the ways you have been like Martha while pursuing your purpose. How can you become more like Mary instead?

Time to Act

SCRIPTURE

And he said to them, "Go into all the world and proclaim the gospel to the whole creation." *Mark 16:15 (ESV)*

DEVOTIONAL

Our purpose is what God placed us on Earth to do. Our purpose is the reason why we are born—born into a specific family, culture, and born for such a time as this (Esther 4:14). Our purpose is what gives our life meaning and direction. Our purpose is what brings glory and reverence to the Most High.

Now that we have wisdom, knowledge, and understanding of God's purpose for our lives, what comes next? What do we do? Where do we go? How do we actively glorify God through our purpose?

Discerning our next steps in our journey will be key to making meaningful and purposeful use of our gifts. God's purpose for our lives is universal. We ought to bring glory to Him using our individual skill sets and talents also known as spiritual gifts.

God will call us to specific assignments to fulfill His heavenly agenda. Some are called to preach; others are called to teach. Some are called to provide physical care, while others focus on matters of the heart and mind. Our calling may require us to work with our hands, while others rely on our knowledge, intellect, and compassion. When we understand who we are and why God created us, we can act on what He's called us to do—the work for which we are gifted.

Our identity and purpose equip us to complete the good works that God saw fit for us (Ephesians 2:10). The works that will spread the good news that Jesus Christ died for our sins for us to be free to love Him, worship Him, and fulfill His purpose for the Kingdom.

REFLECTION

Our Black Girl Magic is what makes us stand out. It's what makes our walk with Christ so special. But it's what we do with our magic that matters most. Are we glorifying God with what makes us so unique? Are we using the many skills and talents gifted to us to love Him, serve Him, glorify Him, and help others come to know Him?

Take some time today to reflect on who He made you to be, and let Him give you wisdom in knowing how best to use those gifts for His glory.

Grab your journal and write down what God has called YOU to do. Don't just write down what you WANT to do or what someone else thinks you should do—write down the things that feel right in your heart and soul, even if those things don't seem practical or possible right now.

Then take a few minutes each day and meditate on these words: "God has called me to do...." Read these words over and over until they become part of your identity and spirit!

Part 3

Calling

Get Ready, Get Ready, Get Ready

SCRIPTURE

And you, Solomon my son, know the God of your father and serve him with a whole heart and with a willing mind, for the Lord searches all hearts and understands every plan and thought. *1 Chronicles 28:9 (ESV)*

DEVOTIONAL

Oh to be called by the Most High! It's exciting. It's an honor that He saw it fit to give us a specific assignment that glorifies Him and blesses others.

But it's also okay to admit that being called by God can be a little frightening. Stepping into something of such magnitude has the ability to make you feel like a mouse attempting to tame a lion. You can find comfort in knowing that David won the victory over Goliath, and you will too!

You may be asking, *How do we know if we are called to something by God? How do we know if it's time to stop thinking about it and start acting on it?* The answer is very simple: we will feel like we are going crazy if we don't listen to that calling.

There's no other way to explain this feeling. It's not a physical sensation, but more so an emotional one. The call is so strong that it's almost impossible to ignore it. Rest assured, God will reaffirm this feeling by speaking directly to your spirit through His Word or wise counsel.

You may try hard to deny or rationalize our calling, especially if it seems far-fetched or out of the norm of what you are used to doing. But if you feel something from within is screaming at you to take action, then it's time to follow your calling.

Doing so is an act of obedience! Start now because delayed obedience is still disobedience in God's eyes.

REFLECTION

Pray this prayer, meditate, and allow God to speak to you. Write down what He reveals pertaining to your calling. Did He confirm what He has already been telling you? Did He reveal something new to you? Write about your experience.

All powerful and equipping Father,
I am filled with gratitude and humility that you think enough of me to call me to your works. Trust in me to reveal your vision for my life. Make clear to me the steps you would have me take. Help me respond without hesitation. I declare that no matter how big or small the assignment, I will operate with a spirit of excellence so that others may come to know you and burn with desire for you. In Jesus's name,
Amen.

Special Delivery

SCRIPTURE

There are different kinds of spiritual gifts, but the same Spirit is the source of them all. There are different kinds of service, but we serve the same Lord. God works in different ways, but it is the same God who does the work in all of us. *1 Corinthians 12:4–6 (NLT)*

DEVOTIONAL

When God calls us to an assignment, He has already considered what it will take to complete our assignments. He proactively equipped us with the skills and talents needed to do His good works.

If we have learned anything thus far, it's that God's craftsmanship of our lives is intentional and well thought out. Just like our identities and purpose, God knew exactly what gifts we would possess to become doers of His Word and walk in His purpose.

When we talk about our spiritual gifts, we are talking about the things God has made us to do in a particular way. Spiritual gifts are far more than a special talent or skill we have acquired over time. Instead, they are predestined, divine abilities for us to take on a particular role and function within the Kingdom.

Our spiritual gifts empower our calling. They are natural talents and skills God gives us to fulfill our God-assigned mission. So, we must tap into and develop our gifts. We don't want to embark upon an assignment ill prepared and ill equipped because we failed to explore our gifts. Learn more about them, then improve upon them.

A deep dive that explores our spiritual gifts is so beneficial for the Kingdom and for ourselves as Black Christian women. Discovering our gifts gives us a deeper sense of self; therefore, we grow and build intimacy with the one who created us. We also make sense of our purpose, which gives us the confidence we need to walk boldly into our God-given calling.

The self-awareness and fearlessness we acquire by tapping into our gifts serves as a witness to anyone we encounter, especially those little Black girls watching and learning from us!

REFLECTION

As Black women, discovering our purpose and uncovering our spiritual gifts gives us a sense of power and belonging in a world that isn't created for us to thrive. Well, find your seat at the table, and bring everything you have to give with confidence and tenacity!

This week I want you to discover your gifts by researching a spiritual gifts assessment online. Your church community may also offer spiritual gift assessments, so don't be afraid to ask. Complete any test of your choice. If you have already discovered your spiritual gift, take a test anyway to determine if something new reveals itself. After identifying your gift or gifts, take some time to reflect on how you can develop and grow your gifts this year.

Thinking of a Master Plan

SCRIPTURE

We can make our plans, but the LORD determines our steps. *Proverbs 16:9 (NLT)*

DEVOTIONAL

One thing about God is that He is the epitome of the statement, "Lead by example." God will never call us to do something that He hasn't done. It may look different, because of His supernatural power, but we can guarantee He has been there, done that. He is a leader, a creative, a strategist, parent, counselor, craftsman, architect, etc. You name it and He's done it!

God is also a planner. An extreme planner at that! Before setting His purpose for creation in motion, He had a plan. He was very detailed and left no stone unturned when He created the Heavens and Earth, man and woman, you and me!

Now imagine if we took the time to plan for our purpose and calling. What if we were as intentional and detailed with making plans to execute what God has appointed us to do?

Some of us wander through life aimlessly, getting by on a wing and a prayer. That's not God's will for our lives. Proverbs 21:5 tells us that "the plans of the diligent lead surely to abundance but everyone who is hasty comes only to poverty." If we follow God's example by making a plan to fulfill our destinies, we can rest knowing we have a strategy for success and a more fulfilling life.

Since we are not all-knowing as our Heavenly Father, we have to leave room for Him to move as He pleases. However, when God reveals His vision to us, if we write out a spirit-led plan, He will establish our steps (Proverbs 16:9).

REFLECTION

Habakkuk 2:2 tells us to write the vision and make it plain. God will reveal His vision and call on your life to you through prayer and meditation on His Word. This week I want you to find an empty journal in your home, or head to your local dollar store to purchase a notebook. This journal or notebook will serve as your planning journal. In this journal you will record the revelations (vision, your calling, and plans for your next steps) God gives to you in your quiet time or throughout the day. Begin seeking God during the planning stages and allow Him to guide your steps.

Stay Ready, So You Don't Have to Get Ready

SCRIPTURE

So be on your guard, not asleep like the others. Stay alert and be clear headed. *1 Thessalonians 5:6 (NLT)*

DEVOTIONAL

Close your eyes and imagine you are the star on a Hollywood movie set and you hear the director say, "Lights, camera, ACTION."

We don't have to be Hollywood stars to know that when a director says "action," it's time to move! There is so much preparation behind the scenes—hair, makeup, studying lines, rehearsals—so when it's action time, you are prepared to play your role.

When God calls us, it's imperative we are ready and prepared to move! Because when we are not, we risk delay in our pursuit or completely missing a moment of significance in our journey.

In Matthew 25, Jesus tells the parable of the ten bridesmaids awaiting the arrival of the bridegroom to join him at the marriage banquet. Five of the bridesmaids were prepared with enough oil for their lamps to get them through the night, whereas the other five bridesmaids were underprepared without enough oil. As the bridegroom approached in the middle of the night, the five unprepared bridesmaids had to leave to purchase more oil, missing his arrival and entry into the wedding banquet.

The girls who get it, get it, and the girls who don't, don't! We don't want to be the daughter who is not ready and prepared when God presents His calling to us. Because when God calls us, He has a job for us. He has a plan for our lives, and it's up to us to stay prepared and ready to jump in when the time comes.

When it's time for you to step into your God-given calling, you don't have to be perfect or have all the answers. Just remember that God will be there every step of the way.

REFLECTION

When you stay ready, you don't have to get ready. We don't know the day or the hour when God will call us to something. We don't want to miss an opportunity to bring Him glory because we are unprepared. Write down three things you will do this week to better prepare for your calling. Whether it's studying the focus of a specific scripture, taking a free webinar, or scheduling quiet time with God, GET READY!

Caring for Your Calling

SCRIPTURE

Work willingly at whatever you do, as though you were working for the Lord rather than for people. Remember that the Lord will give you an inheritance as your reward, and that the Master you are serving is Christ. *Colossians 3:23–24 (NLT)*

DEVOTIONAL

Have you ever thought about how much we prioritize and care for our most prized possessions? Protecting and tending to what we most value is second nature to us. We will go to extraordinary lengths to ensure our possession is safe and secure. We may even sacrifice our time and money to take great care of our things.

We should view our calling and assignment in that same light. Our calling is not just something that we have to do, it is connected to who we are and what our purpose is. It's a big deal. And it's not just a big deal for self-gratification, but for the body of Christ as a whole.

Our calling is an invitation to contribute to something greater than ourselves. Therefore, the effort we put into seeking the Kingdom, growing and developing our calling, and serving others through our calling should be unmatched.

When we find value in what God has ordained for us, we approach the assignment differently. There's a certain seriousness that comes with venturing into an assignment with a high level of value. We should protect our calling at all costs. Do not allow any old distraction or chatter to come against your destiny. Be intentional about growing and developing your skills and talents. And don't be afraid to walk away from the things that threaten your Kingdom assignment.

Our calling is not first come, first serve. God deemed you worthy of it for a divine purpose. The least we can do as His children is show up in full force and honor the gift He has laid before us.

Jesus said, "The harvest is plentiful but the workers are few" (Matthew 9:37). That means there's plenty of work to be done, but not enough people doing it. Therefore, if God has called you to do something, don't ignore it. Take your calling seriously!

REFLECTION

When we find value in the assignment God has called us to, we will stop at no lengths to see it through and perform with excellence. With anything we do in our lives, we should do unto the Lord. Just picture Jesus sending you an email requesting you to complete an assignment or project. You would more than likely drop everything you were doing and be as efficient as possible in getting the job done.

In the space below, answer the following prompt: What do I value and enjoy most about the works God has called me to? This includes day-to-day functions like your job, cleaning your home, taking care of an elderly parent, and parenting.

Bigger than Me and You

SCRIPTURE

Therefore, go and make disciples of all the nations, baptizing them in the name of the Father and the Son and the Holy Spirit. *Matthew 28:19 (NLT)*

DEVOTIONAL

Last week, we learned that God has called us to something greater than ourselves. We exist solely to glorify Him, and whatever our calling is, it will be for the purposes of His Kingdom.

God wants you to love and enjoy your calling. He wants you to be enthusiastic about it and value it so you can show up with excellence. But your calling is not about you. Your calling is about loving God, serving Him, and spreading the good news with the intention of ushering others into His presence, so they will know Him as well.

We all have people depending on us to embrace and walk boldly into our calling. Whether it's family, friends, colleagues, someone we are discipling, or complete strangers, we all have someone we are responsible for bringing into the Kingdom.

There is this story of a man, a young preacher, whom God led to invite his atheist friend to his church's Easter services. The preacher's friend declined the offer, and the two began to debate the existence of Jesus Christ. The preacher stood his ground and witnessed to his friend, then the two parted ways. The preacher wondered why God would lead him to extend an invitation and witness to a known atheist. It seemed like a waste of time to him.

Well, just a few years later, a man walked up to the preacher and thanked him for bringing him to Christ. The preacher was confused because he did not recognize the man. He asked the man to explain how he helped bring him to Christ. The man shared that a few years ago he was doing maintenance work at a building and overheard the preacher witnessing to his atheist friend. The man said he went home that day and told his wife they were going to church for Easter. From that day forward, the man, his wife, and their children were saved.

The preacher's atheist friend was not his assignment after all. It was the eavesdropping maintenance man. The blind obedience of a man led to the salvation of an entire family. Now this family can witness to those assigned to them. This family is now in position to do good works and walk in their purpose and calling.

The work is bigger than us! We are just vessels used by God to fulfill His plan and purpose.

REFLECTION

According to Matthew 28:19, after the resurrection of Jesus Christ, He commissions the disciples to go out into the world and make more disciples. They were instructed to spread the good news in all the nations and baptize people in the name of the Lord. This was not just instruction for His chosen twelve, but for us as well.

God's desire is that everyone comes to know Him. Whether they choose to follow is up to them, but His plans are that everyone be made aware!

So, grab a sheet of paper and write a prayer of salvation for someone you know. Surrender yourself to God in this prayer, and be used as a witness whether by your words or actions. Pray the Holy Spirit softens their hearts so that they will come to know the truth of Jesus Christ.

False Evidence Appearing Real (FEAR)

SCRIPTURE

Have I not commanded you? Be strong and courageous. Do not be afraid; do not be discouraged, for the LORD your God will be with you wherever you go. *Joshua 1:9 (NIV)*

DEVOTIONAL

The Oxford Language Dictionary defines fear as "an unpleasant emotion caused by the belief that someone or something is dangerous, likely to cause pain, or a threat." *Merriam-Webster* defines fear as "an unpleasant, often strong emotion caused by anticipation or awareness of danger."

Fear is debilitating. Fear is paralyzing. God knows the power of fear, which is why He instructs us "do not be afraid" 365 times through the Bible. He knows and understands our fears of the unknown, or fears of failure. He understands the fear of tackling something that seems impossible and the fear of our insecurities. But we are still called.

Fear is a natural human emotion, but it is just that—an emotion. Fear can only thrive if we give it the power to do so. We often allow fear to control our lives. It will dictate what we will and will not do, which can be the very thing that keeps us from our purpose and calling.

It's okay to feel fearful, but do not allow it to stop you from what God has called you to do. We overcome our fears by doing it (whatever your "it" is) afraid. We conquer fear by taking that blind leap of faith and reclaiming our courage. Conquering our fear also sends a message to the enemy that he has no reign over our lives. The enemy thrives on our fear because he knows that when we stand in our power, and allow our Black Girl Magic to shine, he's lost this fight.

God promises that His plans are not to hurt us or cause us danger (Jeremiah 29:11). Even in our suffering as believers, God's plan is never to cause harm, but instead to help us reach our full potential. There is so much waiting for us on the other side of fear. Our dreams, hopes, and breakthroughs are on the other side of fear.

Do not be afraid!

REFLECTION

Fear is a mindset that we can conquer by encouraging ourselves and denouncing fear's paralyzing effects.

Affirmations:

Fear is just a block between me and my assignment.

Fear will not exist within me, because that space is designated for God.

God's plans for me to prevail will come to pass.

Authenticity Rules

SCRIPTURE

Do your best to present yourself to God as one approved, a worker who does not need to be ashamed and who correctly handles the word of truth. *2 Timothy 2:15 (NIV)*

DEVOTIONAL

Who's someone you admired as a child and thought to yourself, "I want to be just like her when I grow up?" As children we often adopt the behaviors and mannerisms of someone with great influence over our lives. As we continue to grow, who and what influences our identity changes. And if we're not careful, we'll mistakenly adopt the identity of someone God did not intend for us.

God's calling is made specifically for us and who He created us to be. We are the only ones who possess the perspective, skill set, and wherewithal to complete the assignment created for us. Showing up as someone else will not get the job done.

Our calling requires authenticity—us in our purest form of being. Our talents, skills, flaws, and failures are all necessary in our calling. Those assigned to you need exactly what you have—nothing more, nothing less.

Not to mention, when you stay true to yourself and your God-given identity, God can reveal more about your purpose and calling because He can trust that He's sending out the right woman for the job!

You will undoubtedly continue to grow and change as your journey continues. But you can trust that you are exactly who you need to be to pursue your Heavenly calling in whichever season you are in.

REFLECTION

Trying to be someone else is counterproductive to your future and your destiny.

Your calling was designed specifically for you! You cannot fully operate in your destiny when you lack authenticity. Authenticity may be difficult when we are not grounded in who God has called us to be. When we don't know who we are, we will often find ourselves taking on the personality, characteristics, or mannerisms of someone else.

Ask yourself, "Is this who God has called me to be in order to fulfill His purpose"?

Align with God and tap into who you are by doing these two things:

1. Find out what kind of woman God made you to be—and then embrace it! Ask Him for guidance on how to use your gifts for His glory.

2. Learn about other women who have gone before you. How did they remain authentic to themselves and their calling?

The Trust Walk

SCRIPTURE

Trust in the LORD with all your heart and lean not on your own understanding; in all your ways submit to him, and he will make your paths straight. *Proverbs 3:5–6 (NIV)*

DEVOTIONAL

This walk with God is all about trust. When we trust God, we put our faith in the power of His Word and the wisdom of His plans. We know that there is a divine purpose for our life, and though we may not know it yet, we can rest assured that it will be revealed.

Relying on God completely means we put our ultimate trust in His power and wisdom. His Word is a lamp that guides our steps as we seek Him (Psalm 119:105). He will not lead us astray. If we keep our eyes on Him and diligently seek Him, He will not only reveal His plans to us, but our next steps as well.

We will not always understand God's motives or how He does things. His ways are not our ways. Our calling may seem a little ambiguous. Our next steps may seem inconceivable or insignificant. The path to uncovering our calling may be met with struggles and strife that we are unable to rationalize, like experiencing a tragedy within our home or family, or unexpectedly losing a job.

But God knows! In fact, He's all-knowing. He knows things that we do not and cannot comprehend. He reveals to us what He knows we can handle in the moment. Our job is to trust Him and know that He is doing a work that we wouldn't believe even if He told us (Habakkuk 1:5).

Before Jesus's crucifixion and resurrection, He told his disciples that we would receive the gift of the Holy Spirit. In different versions of the Bible the Holy Spirit is referred to as an advocate, helper, and comforter. The Holy Spirit was left here to guide us in truth and the future. The Holy Spirit gets instructions directly from God and relays them to us. But it's up to us to obey and follow (John 16:12–13). It's up to us to trust the voice of the helper!

God did not leave us to figure out our purpose or calling on our own. He gave us the ultimate resource. If we just trust His plans and His gentle voice, we'll walk in our divine purpose.

REFLECTION

We do not possess the capacity to go through life by ourselves! We do not have the knowledge and wisdom God has. He knows things about the future we cannot see, and things about ourselves we have no clue about! Therefore, we must put our trust in our Heavenly Father to lead us into divine purpose and calling. To build trust in God we must begin with establishing intimacy with Him. Choose a day this week and commit to 24 hours of prayer and fasting. Spend this time with the Word, praying for a trusting relationship with God, and repenting for the times you failed to put your faith in Jesus.

Adore and Obey

SCRIPTURE

But this command I gave them: "Obey my voice, and I will be your God, and you shall be my people. And walk in all the way that I command you, that it may be well with you." *Jeremiah 7:23 (ESV)*

DEVOTIONAL

Many of us grew up in home settings where disobedience was not tolerated. We knew what was expected of us, and we likely set some of those same expectations for our own children and families today.

You are here on this Earth to do something amazing! God has placed a calling on your life, and it is up to you to obey His instructions as you pursue it.

As Black women, we are called by God to be strong, powerful leaders in our homes and communities. We have a unique opportunity to impact the world through our obedience. Whether He is calling us to start something new, or to stop something hindering us from reaching our destiny, our obedience is pivotal when pursuing our purpose.

However, obedience is not always easy. In fact, it can be downright difficult and uncomfortable. And it's quite typical of God to instruct us to do something we simply do not want to do. Whether it's a biblical principle or a specific instruction from God, we often delay obedience. Or we altogether refuse to do what is instructed of us. We fear losing something we love or love to do. We are afraid of what is or is not on the other side of our obedience.

But the truth is, when we are obedient to God—no matter what it costs us—He rewards our obedience with His favor and protection.

Obedience unlocks breakthroughs, freedom, and opportunities that otherwise would be unobtainable. But above all else, obedience shows honor and respect to our Heavenly Father. Obedience is an act of worship, showing reverence to God for being our sovereign ruler. And that alone should be enough!

REFLECTION

Remember that being obedient to God's instructions is part of what makes YOU special. You were created in His image, and now He wants to use your gifts to bless others.

Grab your journal and complete this prompt:

What is one thing God instructed you to do in the last six months that you have not done? What are you afraid of losing as a result of your obedience? How has disobedience negatively impacted you walking in your calling?

Do not make the mistake of thinking you can put off what God is calling you to do until tomorrow. Tomorrow may never come. Move forward in obedience and let God blow your mind while you still have a chance to experience it.

Detours into Destiny

SCRIPTURE

I know, Lord, that our lives are not our own. We are not able to plan our own course. *Jeremiah 10:23 (NLT)*

DEVOTIONAL

Until we enter the pearly gates of Heaven, we will be on this journey with Christ. And if you have traveled anywhere before, then you know journeys can be met with challenges and obstacles like flat tires, getting lost in the middle of nowhere, or delayed flights. Traveling also has upsides, like meeting new people and exposure to new places and things.

As we journey with Christ, detours are bound to happen at some point. This is why leaving room in your plan for God's will is imperative. Sometimes, things just don't go according to how we envisioned them.

But detours aren't always bad! In fact, they can be wonderful opportunities for growth and change that help us tap into our divine potential. God has given us these detours because He knows what's better for us and wants us to trust Him, even when we have no clue what's going on around us.

When we experience detours, we develop patience and learn to trust God's timing. We can problem solve—a skill that may come in handy if we encounter a similar issue in our future. We build community by engaging with believers who may be experiencing similar detours or obtain wise counsel from a seasoned believer that we can now trust as a mentor. We also trust that God-ordained detours are meant for our good and growth because He is a very intentional God.

Don't worry about things getting crazy or overwhelming once you say yes to God's call on your life. He is now in control. He is the ultimate GPS, and when you surrender to His leadership, He'll lead you into your destiny.

REFLECTION

It can be frustrating when plans don't go our way. But there is freedom from the frustration. Pray this prayer of surrender:

Dear God, by whom my steps are ordered,
I surrender my heart, mind, and soul to you. I surrender my plans to you. I make room for you to orchestrate a life that is pleasing and acceptable in your eyes. Help me to trust in your sovereign ways, knowing that you don't send suffering and hardships to harm me. Help me to suffer well, as your Word commands, and trust that your plan is bigger and better.

The Not-So-Ordinary Calling

SCRIPTURE

Not only that, but we rejoice in our sufferings, knowing that suffering produces endurance, and endurance produces character, and character produces hope, and hope does not put us to shame, because God's love has been poured into our hearts through the Holy Spirit who has been given to us. *Romans 5:3–5 (ESV)*

DEVOTIONAL

The sooner we realize that we do not serve an ordinary God, the sooner we will be able to embrace our extraordinary calling.

For many believers, the idea of being called to a particular vocation or mission in life is difficult to comprehend. They see it as something reserved for a select few and not for them. It's easy for some of us to feel like we don't have a calling because we don't see how we fit into God's plan for the world.

The truth is, we are all called to something special. We do not need large platforms to make an impact. We do not need a perfect past to be called. A college degree does not make our calling any less important than that of the person with a doctorate. No matter our season of life, our calling is paramount in bringing God glory.

Our calling is not necessarily our profession or career of choice, though. For some, it's a specific assignment that may or may not have anything to do with your profession at all. For others, God's calling may be where you get to work every day!

God is very strategic about where He places us and who we encounter in this lifetime. Regardless of where or what you are called to, it's important to remember that you are a light in a dark world. Through you and your calling, someone will get to experience Christ and hopefully come to know Him as Abba Father.

REFLECTION

Embracing your extraordinary calling means recognizing and honoring your unique talents, passions, and purpose. It requires a willingness to step outside your comfort zone and pursue your dreams, even in the face of obstacles or criticism. Here are some ways you can become comfortable with your extraordinary calling:

* Focus on your strengths and passions.
* Set challenging but achievable goals.
* Surround yourself with positive and supportive people.
* Practice self-care to maintain your physical, mental, and emotional well-being.
* Take action and don't be afraid to fail or make mistakes.

* Learn from your experiences and use them to grow and improve.
* Celebrate your successes and accomplishments along the way.

By fully embracing your calling, you can tap into a deep sense of fulfillment and make a positive impact on the world. Remember to stay true to yourself, trust your instincts, and never give up on the journey toward your extraordinary destiny.

All You Have to Do Is Say YES!

SCRIPTURE

And I heard the voice of the Lord saying, "Whom shall I send, and who will go for us?" Then I said, "Here I am! Send me." *Isaiah 6:8 (NLT)*

DEVOTIONAL

When we think about our callings, it can seem like there's an enormous amount of pressure involved. So much so that we will avoid it altogether. We delay giving God our "yes" because the thought of carrying out our calling will require more from us than we believe we possess.

There are often two debilitating myths relating to being called and answering our call: 1) We alone are responsible for carrying out our calling and 2) Our lives have to be "perfect" or close to perfection in order to be called.

We have adopted these faulty belief systems thinking that we operate in our own strength, forgetting that we have a helper in the Holy Spirit who orders our steps.

We sometimes don't believe in ourselves and project that lack of self-trust onto God. But the moment we stop viewing ourselves as just human beings and instead as daughters of The Most High, we will recognize that we belong to a greater power and are connected to a greater power source.

We are His vessels for completing good works. He created us specifically for this. When we think we are missing something, we're not. When we think we don't have what it takes, we do! God doesn't make mistakes; He didn't accidentally call you to this purpose.

Our lives do not have to look a certain way, nor do we have to "have it all the way together" to achieve our Kingdom calling. There isn't a list of requirements for believers to be called. We are not called because we are qualified and have all of our ducks in a row. Instead, God qualifies us once we are called. As we continue to build a personal relationship with Him while pursuing our calling, He will continue to give us what we need to mature in our purpose.

All in all, we can't be afraid to go through the process of being called into our purpose because the possibilities are endless with God. The joy and fulfillment we experience after giving God our "yes" is unlike any other.

REFLECTION

Giving God your "yes" means surrendering yourself to His will and following His plan for your life. It means trusting that His way is better than your own and being open to the opportunities and challenges He presents to you. It requires a willingness to let go of your own desires and ambitions and to seek His guidance and direction. When you give God your "yes," you acknowledge that He is the ultimate authority in your life, and you submit to His wisdom and love.

Affirmations:

I joyfully give my "yes" to God, trusting that His plans for me are perfect.

With faith and courage, I surrender my will to God's will, knowing that His love for me is unending.

I choose to follow God's path for my life, confident that He will guide me every step of the way.

By giving God my "yes," I am opening myself up to His blessings and grace.

I am grateful for the opportunity to serve God and others, and I willingly offer my "yes" to Him.

I trust that God will use my "yes" to bring about His greater plan, and I am honored to be a part of it.

My "yes" to God is a reflection of my deep love and devotion to Him, and I am blessed to be His child.

Don't Fear the Unknown

SCRIPTURE

How great is our Lord! His power is absolute! His understanding is beyond comprehension! *Psalm 147:5 (NLT)*

DEVOTIONAL

Attempting to walk in your calling without God is counterproductive. He called you to it; therefore, you will need Him to see you through it. We don't have the full picture; we don't know His entire plan and purpose.

There are things God knows about us and the world that we will never know; and quite frankly, we don't need to know. When you have faith, that means you have complete and total trust in whatever He says and whatever He calls you to as His daughter.

We often get tied up in wanting the answers to everything—wanting the full picture all at once—instead of trusting the Master and His master plan. We add extra weight, pressure, and stress on ourselves by requesting more than we can handle.

In Habakkuk 1:5, the Lord says to Habakkuk, "Look around at the nations; look and be amazed! For I am doing something in your own day, something you wouldn't believe even if someone told you about it." In John 16:12, Jesus says to his disciples, "There is so much more I want to tell you, but you can't bear it now."

God understands our capacity to comprehend His Word and ways. He doesn't reveal everything to us all at once because He understands what we are able to fathom and carry.

Most of us live full lives with many responsibilities. We are chasing our dreams and trying to remain faithful on this walk with Christ. That's a lot! Why stretch our minds past capacity to make sense of something that we are essentially incapable of? God says He is the lamp to our feet because all we need to be concerned with is our next step in the journey. Not the tens of thousands of steps He has before us. He doesn't light the path to our entire lives, and we should be thankful because He is shielding us from what He knows may drive us insane, cause us to fear, or turn our backs on Him.

"God is not a man that he shall lie," (Numbers 23:19) so if He said it, you can believe.

REFLECTION

To question God's promises is only indicative of a lack of faith in His true and living Word. The Serenity Prayer written by Reinhold Niebuhr reads:

> *"God, grant me the serenity to accept the things I cannot change, courage to change the things I can, and the wisdom to know the difference..."*

Niebuhr then adds to the prayer:

> *"Living one day at a time; enjoying one moment at a time; taking this world as it is and not as I would have it; trusting that You will make all things right if I surrender to Your will; so that I may be reasonably happy in this life and supremely happy with You forever in the next. Amen."[2]*

This week, recite this prayer every morning before you start your day. Start training your mind to have trust in the Lord's plans for life.

2 "The Original Serenity Prayer by Reinhold Niebuhr," Proactive 12 Steps, May 27, 2022, https://proactive12steps.com/serenity-prayer.

Above All Else

SCRIPTURE

Seek the LORD and his strength; seek his presence continually! *Psalm 105:4 (ESV)*

DEVOTIONAL

It's not enough to just have a vague idea of what God wants from us. We need specific direction from Him. And that's why the Bible tells us to seek His face , meaning to seek a deeper relationship with Him, and ask Him what He wants us to do (1 Chronicles 28:9). We learn to recognize His voice and instructions the more time we spend building intimacy and seeking God's face. Seeking God for instruction means that we are leaning on Him for wisdom in every area of our lives, asking Him for direction and guidance on how to live out what He has called us to do.

REFLECTION

This week we are doing a little something different. Below are journal prompts for each day of the week. During your quiet time, journal your thoughts and prayers using the prompt for each day. If you don't engage in regular quiet time, this is your week to start. Set aside time that works best for you to complete this week's activities.

These journal prompts will not only help you seek God's face but will help you gain a better sense of where you are on your walk with Christ as it relates to your identity, purpose, and calling.

MONDAY: How can I know God better? What would I like to know about Him? What questions do I have for Him?

TUESDAY: What influences try to steal my God-given identity?

WEDNESDAY: Be still. What is God telling you about your role in fulfilling his purpose?

THURSDAY: What am I doing today that matters for eternity?

FRIDAY: How are you pleasing God in your walk with Him? What area of your life can you do a better job of pleasing God?

SATURDAY: Is there something in your life causing you to avoid God's presence?

SUNDAY: What is your personal mission statement as you continue to walk in your God-given calling? What do you hope to accomplish?

Adjust Your Crown

SCRIPTURE

"Who knows if perhaps you were made queen for just such a time as this?"
Esther 4:14 (MSG)

DEVOTIONAL

When we say Black Girl Magic, we are referring to the power and grace of us Black women. As Black Christian women, we have displayed strength, resilience, and creativity throughout history and are able to use that magic within ourselves to pursue our God-ordained callings in life.

As Black women, we have so much potential we can tap into once we understand that God made us with an incredible purpose in mind. We are brilliant and valuable and worthy of pursuing our dreams. We deserve to live out our purpose and calling in this world!

We should be on a mission to be an ambassador for Christ by celebrating and nurturing the uniquely amazing attributes He has blessed us with.

We can start by reciting positive affirmations, celebrating what makes us unique.

Sometimes it feels like no one sees or acknowledges our light—that it's hard for people to understand what makes us special. But remember, if we can't see ourselves shining brightly, others will have difficulty seeing our light as well. Speaking God's Word over ourselves and speaking life into our purpose and calling reminds us of who we are and who we serve. Let's affirm what is uniquely amazing about us physically, mentally, spiritually, and professionally.

We can also excel in our personal and professional development. Being obedient to where God is leading us will bring the peace and abundant life that God promises. Go out and get the degree, start the business, schedule the therapy appointment, and grow closer to God. Our future selves will thank us for it!

We've all heard the saying, "You are a product of your environment." What if we flip that to say we are also the ones who can create our environments? Our surroundings greatly impact our progress. Let's aim to dwell where we are loved, spurred, supported, and celebrated. Our environment should bring out the best in us!

Lastly, but most importantly, remember to always love God, ourselves, and those around us. It's God's will for us to love, worship, and serve Him (and others).

REFLECTION

Black Girl Magic is not just a term of endearment but a community! We are stronger together. And as a part of God's army, love and unity will help push forward the legacy of Black Girl Magic for generations to come.

This week let's celebrate and support other Black girls doing their thing! Reach out to as many Black women as you can to give them a compliment, celebrate a recent success, or encourage them using the Word of God!

Prayers for Identity, Purpose, and Calling

SCRIPTURE

Call to me and I will answer you, and will tell you great and hidden things that you have not known. *Jeremiah 33:3 (ESV)*

You made it through the year! Congratulations, sis! God honors your commitment to your relationship with Him and your spiritual growth. Let's round the year out in prayer as you press on to a more bold, proud, God-fident YOU!

PRAYER FOR IDENTITY

Dear Heavenly Father, my creator. God, you did not make any mistakes when you made me. Help me to posture my heart in such a way that I receive and embrace the identity you created specifically for me. Give me a clear vision to see myself the way you see me. Lord, because I was created in your image, may I always remember that the truth of your Word reigns supreme over the attacks of the enemy. Although he comes to distort my perception of myself, I declare that I stand and walk boldly as your daughter, as a royal priesthood, as the one whom you bought at a high price. Father, forgive me for the times I allowed the world to influence the way I see myself. May others always see your light in me. In Jesus's name, amen.

PRAYER FOR PURPOSE

Dears precious King of kings. I surrender my plans to you, that your Kingdom come and will be done. I am honored that you have included me in your plans to build and expand your Kingdom. Father, bless me with a renewed heart, mind, and vision that aligns with the purpose you have set for me and not the one I have created myself. God, use me to bring glory to your name so that everyone attached to me comes to know you as our Lord. May your Kingdom shine light on all the darkness of the world, exposing and tearing down anything that is not of you! Prepare me to fearlessly stand up against what threatens your ultimate purpose. In Jesus's name, amen.

PRAYER FOR CALLING

Dear Most High, thank you for creating a space for me to serve your Kingdom. I pray that you reveal to me the needs of those around me and how I can use what you have blessed me with to meet those needs. God, help me to recognize and appreciate the gifts you have bestowed upon me. I have acquired a heart of obedience and trust in your Word and your direction. May my flesh be sensitive to the Holy Spirit's voice and gentle guidance. God, less of me, and more of you as I confidently walk this calling and inspire others, especially Black girls and women, to do the same. For your glory! In Jesus's name, amen.

CLOSING REMARKS

As the years go on, Black women continue to break barriers, letting the world know, "We are here! We have been here! And we are not going anywhere!" We are demanding respect and can delight in the increase of our representation in media, politics, and all walks of life. We all possess Black Girl Magic. To keep the movement alive, we must nurture what God has given to us.

No longer are we going to be limited by other people's definitions of beauty, success, or greatness. As God continues to develop our self-acceptance and love, we will recognize that our purpose is a force to be reckoned with. By living an authentic life, we will accept our place as cocreators of our story and recognize that no one can ever take away our identity, for it was created and nurtured by God.

As Black women, we must acknowledge the unique gifts that are within us. We must realize our strength is far greater than what anyone tells us. With The Father, The Son, and The Holy Spirit, we can achieve anything we desire. We must break the boundaries of self-doubt and remember that we are valuable and worthy of walking boldly in our purpose and calling.

ACKNOWLEDGMENTS

There are countless people I would like to thank for their support and encouragement throughout my life and the process of writing this devotional. But I'd be remiss to start with none other than God himself. In 2019, God swept me up in a wave of love and grace that forever changed my relationship with Him and my life. I am nothing apart from God. Every opportunity that I am given to share His good works is all a part of God's master plan. Father, it is my prayer that you be glorified through the messages in this book. If I had 1,000 tongues, I couldn't thank you enough.

Secondly, I'd like to thank my number-one fan, my mama. Thank you, Mama, for always cheering me on in everything I do. I am who I am because you never let me forget WHOSE I am. Blessed cannot describe the good work God did when He gave me you. To my daddy, thank you, Big C, for always holding it down for me. I'm incredibly grateful that no matter what I needed during this process, you always came through.

To my three very best friends, Whitley, Porsha, and Javana, your constant support and recognition through my new journey in life means the world to me! I'm so happy to make you all proud. To my 2819 Church squad, led by the fierce Alexes G., y'all have become my sisters and my greatest source of inspiration while writing this devotional. God gave you to me as a reminder of who I'm writing this devotional for—strong Black women who're after God's own heart, committed to this walk of loving Him and making more disciples. I will love you forever.

Thank you to my siblings and extended family. Your love and support never go unnoticed. I am in constant prayer that God continues to cover you and shower you with His unconditional love.

And last but not least, thank you to the incomparable Cannon Ryan Walters, my son and the greatest extension of me. You keep me at the feet of Jesus, son. I came to know God's love because of you. I knew that this motherhood journey would be nothing without God. And I truly believe that, as a result of my surrender to Him, He gave me the absolute best kid to ever walk the face of this Earth. I hope Mommy makes you proud, and I love you beyond words, Cannon.

ABOUT THE AUTHOR

Chelsea La'Nere Brown is an Atlanta-based faith blogger who, at the height of the pandemic, began sharing both her spiritual and self-discovery journeys online. Her blog aims to inspire Christian women to become intentional about their spiritual and personal growth while on the journey to becoming their best selves. Chelsea is also the founder and owner of Chelsea La'Nere, a product-based business that helps Christian women create and maintain faith-based routines and practices that foster spiritual growth, an intimate relationship with God, personal development, and mental wellness.

When Chelsea is not blogging and empowering Christian women, this native of Savannah, Georgia, is a social worker, daughter, sister, friend, and the busy mom of an amazing little boy.